WHY

PRIESTS

LEAVE

"Wherefore a man shall leave father and mother, and shall cleave to his wife, and they shall be two in one flesh."

Genesis 2:24

"Where the inalienable right to marriage and procreation is lacking, human dignity has ceased to exist."

The Development of People, Pope Paul VI

WHY

PRIESTS

LEAVE

The Intimate Stories of Twelve Who Did

Edited by

Father John A. O'Brien, Ph.D.

Hawthorn Books, Inc.   Publishers   New York

First Edition: 1969

CONTENTS

1

AN UNUSUAL BOOK

by John A. O'Brien

Some time ago I received a letter from a New York publisher. "A number of priests," he wrote, "have requested me to ask you to bring out a book on the general theme of why priests leave. This is a subject of widespread and intense interest, with newspapers reporting almost daily the resignation of a priest from the ministry, usually followed by the story of his marriage.

"As the number of departing priests is constantly increasing and that of seminarians is steadily decreasing, the theme suggested surely needs frank and honest discussion if the Church in America is to be spared the calamity which is taking place in Latin America. There millions are dying without the sacraments each year, and the Church is faced with nearly total collapse because of an extreme shortage of priests."

The invitation somewhat startled me. While I understood and appreciated the cogency of the publisher's reasoning, I was concerned that readers might misconstrue the purpose of such a book as an encouragement of defections from both the priesthood and the Church.

Obviously I could not be a party to any such enterprise. I love the Church as a son loves his mother. Though a priest for more than fifty years, I still stand in awe before the sublime dignity of the holy priesthood and in wonderment that our great High Priest, Jesus Christ, had

1

seen fit to share with me His eternal priesthood. As St. Chrysostom points out, there are not two priesthoods, but only one. Thus every priest is a participant of the priesthood of Christ, who resides in a special manner in the heart and mind of every priest, and speaks through his lips and ministers with his hands.

Furthermore, the chief thrust of my long ministry has been to share the precious treasure of our holy faith with others. By voice and even more by pen I have proclaimed its Gospel. *The Faith of Millions,* written over a period of eighteen years, has entered over a million homes and been translated into many tongues. Six volumes, in which pilgrims to our holy faith tell the moving stories of their pilgrimage, have I edited. Some forty bishops have privileged me to assist them in launching diocesanwide and even provincewide crusades to reclaim the lapsed and to bring churchless souls into the great household of the faith.

Hence it was that I wrote the publisher, thanking him for the invitation and explaining why I felt that I could not see my way to accept his invitation. "I cannot afford," I wrote, "to be associated with any undertaking which might easily be misconstrued as encouraging defections from either the priesthood or the Church."

Then occurred a development which radically changed the whole picture. The United States hierarchy decided to sponsor a thorough, systematic study of the problems and new conditions confronting the Church. These stemmed largely from the ferment of ideas unleashed by Vatican Council II and the new openness which it brought to the universal Church. Since the Reformation in the sixteenth century the Church had been operating as if it were under a siege. The drawbridge had been raised and the defenders of the fortress were keeping their powder dry and their guns loaded.

Among the subjects which would be studied with great care, it was announced, would be those affecting the life and ministry of priests. Paramount among these, of course, are compulsory celibacy and the causes of the large number leaving the ministry.

Thus on January 18, 1968, there was sent to every priest in the United States a letter from the office of the National Conference of Catholic Bishops in Washington, D.C. The letterhead bore the names of Archbishop John F. Dearden, President; Archbishop John J. Krol, Vice-President; and Bishop Ernest L. Unterkoefler, Secretary. Addressed to "Dear Fellow Priests," the letter stated:

The Committee on Pastoral Research and Practice of the Bishops of the United States has constituted a Committee on the Ministry and Life of the Priest, made up of bishops and priests, to begin an intensive study of the problems and opportunities facing the priesthood in the United States. We, the members of this Committee, wish to explain our goals and solicit your help.

We are aware that the many different transitions which are taking place in the American Church reflecting the vast cultural changes in its modern role have created a crisis in the Catholic priesthood, a crisis which could be one either of growth or decline. While we see no grounds for naïve optimism about the future, neither do we see any reason for despair. If the problems are great, so also are the opportunities. The dedication, the enthusiasm, and energy of the American priesthood have always been strong and continue to be strong.

But it would be idle to suppose that the difficulties which arise in our era of renewal can be resolved without careful study and planning. We are therefore embarking on a program of research and discussion looking to the development of a statement about the meaning of the priestly ministry in contemporary America. We do not profess to have clear or easy answers, but we do promise to engage in a study of the highest professional quality towards finding the general outlines of answers. We further promise that our research will be honest, thorough, and as extensive as we can make it.

Our Committee is composed of bishops and specialists in the fields of theology, scripture, spirituality, liturgy, history, psychology, sociology, ecumenism, and pastoral work. Each of these specialists will assemble panels from their own fields composed of priests and laity and will also consult with a wide variety of experts in their disciplines. We welcome suggestions about the scope and purpose of the research from all American priests and we are particularly hopeful that all priests, individual as well as representative groups of priests, will devote attention to our project and submit recommendations for research to us.

We understand the desires of many priests for quick response to the pressing problems they face. We shall work as quickly as humanly possible, but we ask you, our brother priests, to realize that a project of the importance and breadth of the present one cannot be done hastily. We will issue interim reports and statements as soon as it is feasible. We wish to emphasize at the time of our first meeting as a committee, our realization of the importance of the project, our firm intention to see it through to a successful conclusion, and our need for your help and prayers.

The letter then bore the names of the whole Committee on the Ministry and Life of the Priest. They are: John Cardinal Krol, Chairman; Bishop Alexander M. Zaleski, Vice-Chairman; Bishop Alden J. Bell; Msgr. W. A. Bachmann (Spirituality); Msgr. William Baum (Ecumenics); Archbishop John J. Carberry; Bishop James V. Casey; Father Bernard Cooke, S.J. (Theology); Msgr. John Tracy Ellis (History); Msgr. John Egan (Pastoral); Father Andrew M. Greeley (Sociology); Archbishop Paul J. Hallinan; Father Eugene C. Kennedy, M.M. (Psychology); Father Eugene H. Maly (Theology); Bishop Ernest J. Primeau and Father Theodore Stone (Liturgy).

Upon learning of this development, the officers of the National Association for Pastoral Renewal (NAPR) sought an appointment with Archbishop Dearden, the president of the conference. They wanted to learn if the members of the committee were planning on conducting the study of the celibacy problem with closed minds and with the conclusion predetermined.

Accordingly the NAPR officers met with Archbishop Dearden and Bishop Zaleski in Detroit on March 29, 1968, for a frank discussion. Happily they were assured that the study would be conducted by scholars using the techniques of modern social science.

The purpose would not be to bolster a predetermined conclusion but to lay bare the real facts and thus to discover the truth. The study would be an honest one and not a mockery. The jury would not form its verdict until it had heard all the evidence, pro and con.

This was indeed refreshing news. It represented a distinct advance from the old days, when theologians and biblical scholars were told to look only for evidence that would support a predetermined conclusion.

These surprising and unexpected developments completely removed the grounds of my declining the publisher's invitation. To double my assurance, I consulted several senior priests, known for both their scholarship and their dedication to the Church, concerning the prudence and wisdom of my undertaking the project. Their verdict was unanimous.

"Yes," they said, "bring out such a book. It is badly needed. It will afford the bishops an insight into the reasons for more than a thousand priests leaving the ministry in the last two years. Who are in a better position to state the reasons than the priests themselves? Such information will be helpful not only to the bishops but also to the laity. The Church in this country does not consist merely of 235 bishops but of all the People of God. The findings will be of interest and of value to all.

"After bringing out so many books, like *The Road to Damascus,* telling of the journeys of many gifted and brilliant converts, it is high time for you to turn the spotlight on the exodus going out the rear door. Every sincere truthseeker and lover of the Church must be as much concerned with the departures as with the entrances."

Convinced of the truth of what they said, I wrote to the publisher, telling him of the circumstances which transformed my previous negative decision into an enthusiastic affirmative. He was greatly pleased, for he was more concerned with the good which, with God's grace, the book would do than with any other aspect.

Accordingly I formed an advisory editorial committee of scholars—priests and laity—to assist me in the selection of the most suitable contributors. Out of the vast number of priests who had left the ministry in recent years, we sought to find not only good and dedicated men, which would have been easy, but also men with scholarship and literary craftsmanship. Though this was no easy task, we are confident that we have found them.

We explained that we wanted the stories to be told in a clear, straightforward manner that would disclose the real reason for leaving the ministry. Only in this way would we achieve our objective. Since we presumed that love and the desire for marriage would be likely factors in many cases, we requested that these be not bypassed.

As the reader will see, the writers have responded with transparent honesty and candor. They write with a blazing sincerity which never fails to move and which has a simple eloquence all its own. While all would have found it easier simply to lower the curtain on their departures and say nothing, they realize that if the celibacy problem is to be solved in a rational manner, the truths concerning their motives for departing must be disclosed.

Hence they write with a deep sense of dedication to the Church and for the sole purpose of helping it solve this problem in the light of conditions prevailing today and not on the basis of mere tradition or a blind adherence to the customs of the past. Because their stories disclose the operation of their hearts as well as of their intellects, they will appeal to all the People of God. All must participate in some way in determining whether or not the time has come for a change in the Latin rite Church's requirement of a promise of perpetual bachelorhood as a condition for ordination.

I want to acknowledge my indebtedness to the members of my advisory committee, who favored me with invaluable suggestions at every turn. I express my profound gratitude also to the contributors, my brothers in Christ, who, though laboring outside the strictly sacerdotal field, will always remain priests, sharers of the eternal priesthood of Christ. Not even the Church can tear that indelible mark from their souls. That is why the term "laicization" is a gross misnomer and should be speedily replaced by a better word.

The contributors allow us to look at the heart of a priest, torn between conflicting loyalties, and to see the moving drama each experienced as he reached his agonizing decision. Perhaps history will acclaim them blazers of new trails that needed desperately to be made in a jungle cluttered by the tangled growth of centuries.

They have thrown light upon a subject which has been discussed in darkness, but which can be dealt with intelligently only when we know the facts. Hence they deserve the thanks of all the People of God, and every reader will, I am sure, wish to join me in breathing a prayer that somehow, someday, we all shall meet in the city not made by human hands, eternal in the heavens.

2

LOVE FINDS A WAY

by Kenneth E. Killoren

Kenneth Edward Killoren was born in Charleston, South Carolina, on May 31, 1919. He received his B.A. and M.A. degrees from St. Louis University. After completing his theological studies at St. Mary's College, St. Marys, Kansas, he was ordained on June 17, 1953.

He completed his tertianship in Decatur, Illinois, from 1954 to 1955. In September of that year he was sent to Korea to prepare for the establishment of Sogang College in Seoul and served as its first president from 1957 to 1963. For the following three years he served as dean of student affairs and then was appointed president of Daegun College, Kwangju, Korea. Kenneth Killoren returned from Korea September 1, 1967, and the following November applied for laicization.

The dispensation from all the obligations of the priesthood and the religious vows was received on July 15, 1968, and on August 30 he was united in marriage to Jo Anne Lee. He is now an associate in the development department at the Illinois Institute of Technology in Chicago.

To ask why I left the priesthood first demands an answer to why I joined the priesthood, and to answer that, I must go back thirty years and more. I wanted to do a work on this earth that had a surefire eternal effect. I thought the priesthood was the best and most direct way to achieve this, which it is; but as I lived my priestly life, I began to see more and more that other great works and other states of lives have tremendous eternal potency.

But the question, Why did I leave? To draw more spiritual or eternal effect out of a new state of life? No, nothing so grand as that. The question of my leaving is often put to me like this: What went wrong? Where did I fail? Why did I lose my way? I shouldn't have looked back once I had made my choice. I shouldn't have fallen in love with a mere girl after having loved God as a priest. I shouldn't belong to any woman once I had belonged to the Church.

This is the way I am often approached in reproach, especially by those sorrowful-eyed Catholics who do not condemn openly but only with their eyes. They cannot get over the shock and surprise and cannot admit the possibility that a strong, positive reason was at work in my soul all through this change.

Who knows when and how it all began or came about, either the road into the priesthood or the road out? The road out is freshest in my mind. These thoughts came every year of my life, many times: Am I leading the fullest life I can lead? Is it the life I want to lead? Am I fulfilling my being? Am I loving and living positively or merely avoiding trouble?

Each time for years and years I had answered myself with a hearty Yes and plunged into more and more work to scrub out those lingering doubts. To be too tired to think was a blessing of a sort, I thought. But you cannot pull your heart in two directions and still go one path in life. Finally it had to be resolved.

No one had suspected, not family, not friends, not even unfriendly eyes. I often wondered why they didn't see the doubt in my face and the hesitation in my heart. I expected others to know what I was unwilling to tell. I had fooled them long enough. Now it was really hard to find someone to talk to. Who would believe I was in love? Surrounded by priests day and night, I was afraid to discuss the innermost secrets of my heart. We never spoke of the most important and the most personal things to each other. Whether it was lack of trust or lack of courage, I don't know, but I just never got in there and let my hair down to one of my own priest brothers.

With no excuse left, I pushed myself through the door of my confessor's room. He was a saintly old Columban father in Kwangju whom I admired. I knew what he would say and he said it, kindly but with strong opposition. We fought it out several times and his opposition strengthened my resolve. I loved this girl and would love her in the future, but just how was not clear to me. I would not give her up. If necessary, I would give up the priesthood first. If I could have both the priesthood and Jo Anne, I would be happy with both. But I knew there was still no way to be an active Latin rite priest and an active husband, too. I had read every paper and magazine that came into the seminary to find some Church answer, but none appeared.

It was a matter of importance of loves, which one came first, then which came second or third. I put down on a piece of paper one day these important loves in my life: first, God; second, His Church; third, the priesthood; fourth, the Jesuit Order; and fifth, Jo Anne. I wrote this to Jo Anne and told her I loved her but she must remain fifth behind all the others, but in front of a thousand other loves of friends, relatives, sports, food, and the rest. In the list, she had the first place among all humans but not among all persons, since God was the most important person. But somehow, God as Person was more a philosophical reflection than a live, real, breathing, thinking, reacting being.

I never felt a person-to-person relationship to God. He was a great superb being, not person like I was a person but a kind of Super-Person. All the distinctions in the world of philosophy and theology that had been drummed into my head couldn't wipe away that unfathomable difference for me.

As my love of Jo Anne grew, I told myself and her that I would leave the Jesuits for her, and still, if I could remain a priest, keep her and the priesthood, too. I thought I could somehow keep both seemingly opposite loves, the love of a woman and the love of priesthood. They didn't really seem opposite, but I didn't see how they were mutually nonexclusive in this day and age.

For the time being, Jo Anne accepted this position, and I kept reading and thinking about how I could sanctify both states at once, as a married priest. Could I join the Orthodox? No, I was convinced my Church was the one Christ founded, though I conceded that the

Orthodox was very close to it in shape and form. Could I be an Angli-
can or an Episcopalian? Both allowed married clergy as a Church-given
right, but I was in doubt about their whole setup and didn't want to
complicate an already complicated situation.

So I placed Jo Anne firmly ahead of the Jesuits on my list of loves
and waited for the day to carry out my self-removal from their body.
I loved the Society of Jesus as a group of men that fiercely fought for
a noble cause. I met hundreds of marvelous guys in it. Many I admired.
Most I liked. Some I merely tolerated. But they could get along without
me very well indeed. For twenty-seven years I had given my all to their
type of service, and I had received back much more than I had given.
I had held the highest positions of the Society on local levels and found
these places of honor and authority only weary and burdensome.

I was never asked if I would like to take these high positions. I was
always told to take them, even after protest and complaint. Good old
Ignatian obedience. Do your darnedest, try your hardest, and somehow
you will succeed, I was advised. God won't ask you what you did but
why you did it, so try, try, try. Trying is all right, but there must be a
proportion of ways and means and the end must seem possible and
attainable.

As we struggled on at Kwangju, I had already put Jo Anne's love
ahead of the love of the Jesuits. Now I saw the priesthood itself in a
new light. As rector of the second major seminary in Korea, I was responsible for bringing young Koreans to the fullness of flower as future
priests of God in Korea. I should have refused that job with all my
heart.

Every few days, I wrote to Jo Anne in Seoul, pleading my love,
learning her every thought, and writing reams of pages of letters to try
to express my new heart to her. She was in the fourth position and
growing stronger. If I could not have her and the priesthood, and it
seemed impossible that I could have both, then which would prevail:
love of priesthood and continued acceptance of celibacy, or love of
Jo Anne and forgetting about celibacy?

All winter long my heart tried to hold both loves fully. I tried to see
what was needed for my seminarians, and yet I often raced to Seoul to
be near my beloved Jo Anne. Once in January 1967 she came to live
at the seminary with a group of six Koreans and forty Americans. She

was one of the Korean instructors of Korean language to those Peace Corps members. We had rented our empty rooms and buildings to them for their language work. It was vacation time for us, during those cold months.

We were both busy all day with our separate work, but we spent long hours each night talking together. How could we solve the two loves in my heart? Jo Anne had only one love, love of me, and tried to understand my constant chatter, without reserve but without solution, about loving her and priesthood both.

She returned to Seoul again to plunge into the agony of despair of getting my full love. She had to play second fiddle to priesthood, and she proposed the "hidden flower in my heart" theory. She would go on unmarried, loving me secretly, being second, while I would go on as a priest openly, loving her secretly and second to priesthood.

In March I finally had a knee operation for removal of loose bodies in the right knee. School had just started and the boys came over to the little Korean hospital to care for me. Jo Anne also came down from Seoul, and we ended up with three of us sleeping away in the small room, a seminarian on my left, and Jo Anne on my right. She slept in her slacks.

In April I finally got off the crutches and began an active life of traveling around seeing bishops who seldom came to see us. Within three days I had to go back to Kwangju. The nasty knee was ballooning up and I could hardly sleep again. A second operation was called for, and so on May 1, I again went to the same small private Korean hospital. This time my mind kept grinding away at one thought: Shall I give up the priesthood and get permission to marry Jo Anne? Long nights alone trying to read the shadows on the ceiling gave me no rest. Finally one morning, I sat up in bed, just a mat on the floor anyway, and took out a piece of paper and wrote: "Dearest Darling Jo Anne: This is a letter you shall never forget. I am asking you to marry me after I get the permission from the Church. Please take your time in answering. I will wait a year or two if you need that much time. I hope you don't."

I didn't say "if" I get the permission, for I was certain I would get it if I used every power and means to get it honorably. I didn't say "when" I get permission because time was not the important thing. I was going to get it, and I was going to marry the one I loved after I got permission. There wasn't even a shadow of a doubt that the Church would grant me my request.

I did not know whether Jo Anne would accept my proposal of marriage or not. Her love of me was well known and clear to me, but the difficulties that lay ahead might scare her off or make the price too great to pay. But I thought she would accept, and I pleaded my proposal gently and firmly in the months following.

She was now clearly in third place, ahead of Jesuits and ahead of priesthood. I loved her more than I loved the priesthood as priesthood was held in the Latin rite of the Catholic Church, as a required celibate state.

The knee slowly healed and I was again on crutches for weeks and weeks. Jo Anne had come one night during the second hospital stay, a few nights before I wrote my letter of marriage proposal. She was now busy with her June final exams and could come to Kwangju only once more before I could walk again. She stayed in a hotel, and I went down to see her on my crutches and we even went up into the hills for a picnic, me still on crutches. It was a delightful day.

Finally in late June the boys left for home and summer vacation, and we, the faculty, started a five-day self-study of our program, policies, manpower, etc., at Kwangju. I was busy as chairman of all these meetings and fervently poured myself into them for the good of Daegun College Seminary. On the last day of the sessions, in early July, I received the long-awaited letter from Jo Anne: "Yes, I accept your loving proposal of marriage. Yes, we will marry. I can hardly contain my happiness and can hardly wait to see you in Seoul and hear your words of acceptance."

The Jesuit world was a very busy one those hectic July days of 1967. We had a retreat planned in Seoul where all the Jesuits in Korea would attend and we would talk about our Jesuit community life. I was enthusiastic about the project all along and entered into the preparations and the discussions with a gusto that surprised me, me who was planning to leave the Jesuits and the priesthood.

I arrived a day early in Seoul and spent it all at Jo Anne's room. What a loving and long embrace we had. We repeated our promises of love and marriage and waiting for the permission of the Church. We put rings on each other's fingers with words of promise of marriage.

We had former class rings and they served as engagement rings. In my heart, that was the marriage itself, needing only the Church's blessing of it, so sure to come someday. We remained close all day. We tried to foresee every difficulty and trouble ahead. And it didn't seem hard or impossible at all. It was a day of great advance in our love.

There were many other events in July that are important; a trip to offshore islands with Jo Anne and her close friend; daily letters from our east-coast summer camp; then back to Kwangju via Seoul and, of course, a visit to Jo Anne. By this time, my love of her so possessed me that I hated to go to Kwangju. I hoped to start off the semester, slowly unfolding my plans to my superiors, carefully arrange my changeover and getting a new rector, and thinking this could all be done in six months' time.

I had not reckoned with my foolish heart. In early August on the way to Kwangju via Seoul I openly entertained the idea of forgetting the long and glass-strewn road ahead—announcing all my plans to un-suspecting superiors, seeking and carrying out the request for laiciza-tion, and waiting for the Church to act. I was tempted to ask Jo Anne to marry me right then according to Korean law and to let the Church catch up with me, rather than to wait for it to fulfill the iota of its laws in my regard.

Maybe Jo Anne had moved into number-two spot, ahead of Church? Would she ever get to number-one spot, ahead of God Himself? I shuddered at the thought but it was real. Would I ever dare to take Jo Anne ahead of God and put her, a creature like me, ahead of and above Him, the Creator? No, it didn't seem possible or necessary.

And what about Holy Mother the Church? She would seem more like Crabby Sister the Church, upset at another priest asking out of the celibate rule, and knowing no other way out, asking out of the whole show.

It seemed to Jo Anne and I that we had the faith and the strength to keep our love of God and of the Church above the love of mere self and above the love of each other and we would submit to its rule. Such an act of faith in God and in His Church we had never made before and it cost us much.

Down in Kwangju, in the heat of August, in the burden of work and the rush of preparation for the new semester, I was getting close to my zero line of endurance. Sleep was impossible. Peace of mind was a

million miles away. My confessor had been left far behind at the first
knee operation after his hour-long tirade about how wrong I was, how
foolish, how silly.

"Wait till you see her in the morning all full of curlers, she won't be
so beautiful then. Wait till she gives you the old silent treatment and
you don't know what you did wrong when to whom. Wait till you see
the trials and pains of married life. You'll wish you never left the
priesthood and you'll wish you were back." He was a superb preacher,
pulling out all the stops and missing no arguments. Mostly I loved him
for his own fierce love of the priesthood and for saying that he'd sooner
die than go back on the promise to God to live until death without a
wife.

I didn't feel that way, and rather than cause him further pain, because I was going my way for sure, I said good-bye and never went
back. But finally, at the seminary, I was fit to burst my insides out.
I had to tell a Jesuit to prepare them for the coming shock. I finally
spilled my plate of beans to a young Jesuit priest on a train ride to
Seoul together. Above the clatter of the wheels and the smell of fish
and sweat, for three hours I squeezed my soul dry to him in brotherly
anguish. When it was all over, I was limp and ready for his blows. But
no blows came, to body or to soul. He merely said: "I hate to lose you
as a brother in Christ but go and tell your superior at once and get on
with your plans. If you have the courage and perseverance to carry
them out, it will be proof enough of your sincerity and singleness of
purpose."

So within thirty minutes after arriving in Seoul, and within ten
minutes after arriving in the Jesuit Residence at Sogang College in
Seoul, Korea, I was standing at my superior's desk.

"I am sorry to hurt you, John, but I must cause you a great suffering.
I must tell you that I wish to resign from the rectorship of Kwangju,
resign from the Society of Jesus, resign from the active priesthood, and
seek permission to marry Jo Anne." It came out like a gush of water,
like spoken tears.

I could hardly get the words out. My lips and chest seemed to refuse
to work and cooperate. Here I was, the number-two man in Korea
among the Jesuits, telling the number-one man that I wanted out, out
of everything, and in, into that impossible state for a priest, into marriage. He didn't laugh nor did he gasp. He just sat there a few moments

and seriously asked: "Have you thought this over very clearly and have you sought the advice of others?"

I said that I had thought it over for two years and had sought non-Jesuit advice and that advice had all been negative to my proposal, that I shouldn't do it. I said I had insisted on my rights and that I wished to do just what I said.

"Well," Father John Daly said, "let's take a walk after supper. We can discuss it again then."

After supper we walked around the ball field several times, but John had no new arguments, only the old ones of age, race, culture, and personality differences between myself and Jo Anne. He knew her well and liked her as one of his best students. He seemed to admit to himself that I was too stubborn and had already made up my mind fully and there was no point in arguing. He had to speak his piece of opposition, of foolishness, trouble ahead, and his disbelief that I was making a wise move so fast and suddenly.

Next day at nine o'clock in the morning, Father Daly reluctantly announced to the four other members of mission-consultors group (Fathers R. Kelly, Tracy, Pak, and Bernbrock) what I had requested. All other business stopped. We had gathered in Seoul to discuss the manpower crisis at Kwangju and now it was a crisis that was internally made and not a mere shortage of men. What to do with Killoren was the first and only business of the day and days to follow.

I was asked to come to the group at 10:30 that same morning and I did so. I repeated my request simply and plainly. Fathers Kelly and Tracy just looked at the floor. Father Bernbrock tried to be kind with a statement like this: "You must be relieved now to have that off your chest."

It was strange he said "chest" for I could hardly breathe, so paralyzed were my chest muscles. I admitted a kind of relief that comes when one finally stands up in public before legitimate authority and asks that authority to start the procedure that will put one beyond that same authority in due process of time. But there was no relief for the crushing feeling I had in my breast.

All of a sudden, there in that room with those Jesuits, I felt very much alone, as if I were starting a long journey down a glass-strewn path in my bare feet, and yet I was determined to walk it, come what may.

Father Pak asked: "But why do you have to leave the Jesuits?" It needed no answer. I had to leave because I couldn't stay a Jesuit and openly profess and follow my love of the one I loved above any religious institute or human person.

Father Kelly came to my room and suggested I type out formal resignations to the rector's job as the head of the seminary and to the president's job as the head of a Korean college responsible to a board of trustees. I did this quickly and willingly. I was starting to cut the ties openly now.

The mission consultors had only one solution, that I leave Korea as quickly and as quietly as possible. I did not accept this at once but said I must consult with Jo Anne. It was the two of us now, not just one, who must concur on each future act that affected our lives.

I went to her second-floor room at her boardinghouse. She was waiting for me with great anxiety. I told her briefly that I had been asked to leave Korea as soon as possible.

"Do you want to go?" she asked.

"No, of course not. But it will be easier on Sogang College, the Jesuits, and the Catholic Church in Korea if I go. Can you wait for me?" I asked.

In answer she pulled out a letter she had written that day. "If you decide to stay in Kwangju, to stay a priest, to stay a Jesuit, I will understand, but you will never see this letter. If you still wish to do all the things you spoke about for the past six months, then I wish to marry you as a free man after you get your permission and I will spend the rest of my life making you happy as my husband. Only when I see your answer in your face and your strong conviction to go this hard road will I show you this."

I was again touched by this great show of love to me.

"Yes, yes, I will wait even years if necessary," she added in her tears. "You'd better go now and continue to obey until you are free."

I thanked her for her brave answer and reported back to Father Daly. If I had refused, they would have had a real mess on their hands to keep all this out of newspapers and from scandal-spitting mouths.

Many of the acts in the following days seemed to be lacking personal love from my Jesuits. I had never noticed this before. But maybe I should not have expected kindness and help at that time. Still, after twenty-seven years, and lots of years as superior, there seemed to be no thanks but only reproach. The reputation of the Society of Jesus came first and the personal feelings of the men in it came second.

Father Kelly came to my room in the Jesuit Residence to tell me: "I think you have made a crazy decision. Would you be willing to go to see Dr. John Kim, the psychiatrist, at St. Mary's Hospital and just talk to him?" I thought he meant "crazy" in the slang sense but he didn't.

I agreed to go and do it, to make sure I wasn't crazy in my decisions. In my mind, I had agreed to do anything and everything the Jesuits asked me to do in order to prove my loyalty to them and to prove to myself that I was strong enough to overcome every obstacle to my final goal, Catholic marriage with Jo Anne.

I met Dr. Kim a few hours later in his office on the first floor of St. Mary's Hospital. How fast it all seemed to go. This was an emergency, and the Jesuits must have burned up the wires to make the appointment. I was never to see the Jesuit Residence again except for a few hours just before I left on the plane two weeks later.

Since I figured that I was to unburden my soul to Dr. Kim as a part of this arranged plan of my superior to have me checked thoroughly for mental aberrations, I spit out my story to him like a fire hose. He phoned Father Daly and asked if I could be kept at the hospital for a few days of observation. A few days were destined to be two weeks, two weeks of hell at St. Mary's, confined to a large, spacious, very expensive room with toilet, shower, refrigerator, sofa, easy chairs, air conditioner, and two single beds. I was not flattered by the plush quarters.

The parade of pills started at once: little pink balls, yellow capsules, and large round white disks like aspirin. My extra clothing, pajamas, shaving kit, and whatever I had brought up from Kwangju for the meeting in Seoul were brought in to me by Father Daly. He is the only Jesuit I saw during the two weeks in the hospital.

Almost every day for two weeks Dr. Kim came in for a half-hour talk. He was too indirect, roundabout, and sweet to me. It seemed to be the first time he had ever handled a priest in this situation. We had been friends for years, and I knew him well as a teacher at Sogang and as a consultant at Kwangju but never as a doctor treating his patient.

He was always most kind but he was slow to make a judgment about me. I had to ask him what he thought because he always seemed more like a lawyer trying to crack my story than a doctor trying to help me.

"You have made a neurotic decision," he said one day.

"Neurotic? You mean crazy?" I asked back.

"Well, not crazy but not normal," was his answer.

Not normal! My God, how well I knew that, after two years of rubbing my soul raw against the narrow walls of doubts and worries. But neurotic, crazy, abnormal, suspected, confined, observed—I felt like a nut already. If you have never seriously asked yourself if you are crazy and if you have never had a trained psychiatrist tell you to your face that you are neurotic, you have missed a low point in your life.

I decided then and there that no number of pills and no number of arguments could make me waiver. After one week I asked to see Jo Anne and tell her what was happening. She must be out of her mind worrying about me.

"No, that is the worst thing you can do at this time," the doctor said. "You shouldn't be seen going to her house. And you must think this out away from her."

"Unless I get to see her, I will walk out of this hospital, and you have no legal or physical way to stop me," I answered coldly.

"All right, I'll check with Father Daly," Dr. Kim said.

In an hour or so, Dr. Kim came by to say that Father Daly was sending someone over to Jo Anne's house to tell her to come down and see me for an hour.

I do believe that poor Jo Anne half-expected to see me chained to the bed like a raving maniac. I was under heavy sedatives but was very composed. We talked softly and reaffirmed our love and determination to go all the way. These trials were God-given, and we would surpass any and all trials present and ahead.

How I prayed and thought and searched my soul and my life again while in that room. Each morning I went to the cathedral, right next to the hospital, for early Mass and Communion. Soon I learned that the plane ticket and passport and visa were nearly finished and that I would not get back to Kwangju again to pack my clothes and books for my final break with the seminary. I had wished to say good-bye to the faculty and staff. No, I was told that it was better if I didn't come back and upset them. And my desk, my files, my letters, would never be seen again. My personal papers and clothes were all packed up and shipped to Seoul. Not even a chance to straighten up the official papers for the next man. What irony. I felt like a criminal who had been apprehended in mid-crime and had been spirited away to a secret place lest he cause big trouble. What a drastic change had taken place.

It was hard not to be bitter. I knew many of the Jesuits and friends around Seoul had been coming to the hospital trying to see me. No one was allowed in. I was too sick to be seen, it was said, but I was in good hands, so don't worry. After twenty-seven years as a Jesuit and twelve years as a priest in Korea, all I was good for now was to be gotten rid of. It took every ounce of the little loyalty I had left not to walk out that silly, unlocked door and tell the Jesuits to go to hell, and the Church, too, if need be. And God, too, if it had to come to that.

But I could never do it. What I started, I would finish and clean up as clearly and as properly as I could, according to all the rules, with honor and respect.

I felt caught in a corner. There seemed to be no way to go out of the Society of Jesus and out of the priesthood and still keep my respect in others' eyes. To leave was bad, no matter how I left. I had vowed to God. I had made solemn promises. I had accepted all the restrictions. All these had been judged honorable. But to ask out of the vows, the promises, the restrictions, this was dishonorable. You cannot change your mind.

I didn't want to say No to God. I just wanted to say a different type of Yes. My former Yes to God in priesthood and vows was putting a pressure on my soul that made me fear for my eternity. I couldn't go on as a Jesuit and as a priest and keep my own self-respect. Even if I had to sacrifice the respect of others for me, I would do it.

Jo Anne came in one night unexpectedly. She just decided to walk in without asking permission and she did. No one stopped her. No one questioned her. She let her simple heart lead her to my door and we talked for an hour. We again encouraged each other to bravery and patience, to trust in God. We said a few prayers together. I knew then that I could have her and have my Church and my God in nonconflicting loves if I were a layman. It would take time, but I knew I would get free by following proper channels.

I wish I could have remained an active priest. I could not keep that life of priesthood without accepting the burden of celibacy. I wanted to love Jo Anne first and above priesthood, so priesthood had to go. Apparently priesthood has to be first or not at all in the love scale. I didn't fool myself that my love of Jo Anne would be a platonic one. I wanted to join and unite with her in every way possible: in body, mind, soul, house, money, job, recreation, and free time.

Being celibate didn't mean a thing to me to be a better priest. Yes, I could see it for a priest who was a Jesuit, as a member of a special group who freely vowed to live a common life together without a wife and children. But why, then, did I not honor and continue in this vow of chastity as a Jesuit? Did I not choose it as a voluntary thing over and above the obligation of priesthood? So why all this fuss about being forced to celibacy?

I wanted to be a priest first, a Jesuit second, or to be a priest as a Jesuit and not as a diocesan priest. The second vow of chastity was just a strengthening of the agreement to remain celibate as a priest, no more than that. So if I wanted Jo Anne as my wife more than I wanted the no-wife priesthood, I surely wanted her company and love a hundred times more than the superficial love of the Jesuit community.

I knew great times, great joys, great peace, and great graces as a Jesuit. I often wondered in prayer if it was possible for a man to be happier than I, and I didn't think it was possible to be happier than I was as a Jesuit. But in Korea I felt the pressure of a small community. Little differences of opinions became big ones. Even social amenities were often denied to one another. What fraternal love was this? To play cards, to go to the movies, to eat together, were just ways of spending time together harmlessly and at least politely. And too often I saw angers flare and no apologies asked or given. I heard words that came from priestly mouths to other priests that would be condemned in the ugliest of families. I felt a superficial bond of the same work at the same place at the same time as the big bond and no real deep sharing of that work, place, or time.

Coexistence was not enough for me. Love is reciprocal. If I didn't receive it, maybe it was because I didn't give it, or give enough of it, or give it often enough.

I can say against myself that I was not the leader of love in any of the Jesuit communities I lived in. But I was not the last to open the door of my heart and let a little warmth out.

"Of course, we cannot give you the kind of love that Jo Anne gives you," one Jesuit wrote to me while I was in the hospital, "but we do love you and always will."

I would have liked to believe that last part except for the condition that this love would come if I stayed away from Korea and did not return to do serious damage to Sogang College and the Church and Korea. To speak of love while being expelled from Korea was strange.

It was not only the kind of warm, physical, human, close, personal, constant love that Jo Anne gave me that I wanted but the identification with that love in the total sharing through a human arrangement before God and man.

I end where I began, with love. All the love I gave or received for all the twenty-seven years of my previous state of life cannot equal or match the short year of love I have found in a woman like Jo Anne and the short months of love I have found in her as a wife.

I'm glad I left to follow my greater love. I would have been half-happy following a lesser love, but why be half in love? I plead for understanding of the men who follow such a human love even if it leads them away from the daily, strictly spiritual service of God and Church. They are not less good and not less holy. It is too easy to point the finger and say: "He couldn't remain pure; he couldn't control his sexual powers; he was rushed off his feet by a pretty face; he ran away from authority and a hard life; he got the girl in trouble and wanted to avoid greater scandal; he was getting old and wanted to remain young."

Why not say: "Let God judge him. Let his future life be proof of his new convictions even more than his former good life was proof of his former convictions. Let's give him love and understanding as we all hope to be loved and understood when we follow our deepest conscience on a new and singular path."

On September 2, 1967, the morning after I arrived back in my home province in Milwaukee, I had a heart-to-heart talk with my provincial, Father Joseph Sheehan, S.J. We both cried like two dear brothers. He begged me to go slowly and take another month or more before I made my formal application to leave—"handing in my papers" it was called in recreation-room slang. How could I refuse such a plea to think and pray again about staying and working with him and others as a priest and as a Jesuit?

In the meantime I worked on my brother's game farm up north, with permission of Father Sheehan to live outside the cloister of the religious community. It is called exclaustration. After the month was up and Father Sheehan had gone to Korea, Rome, and South America on Jesuit business, we met again. He felt that if I tried the priestly life again, I might regain my taste for it. I said I couldn't do it without telling everybody I worked with that my mind was made up and that I had handed in my papers and was merely awaiting release from vows. He said I should take one more month back at the farm, and if I still thought I must go, he would help me in every way at that time.

Another month of work and prayer and on November 1, 1967, I handed in all my papers of request and reasons to be freed of the obligation of celibacy and of the religious vows. This is what is meant by laicization: to become the same as a layman.

True to his word, Father Sheehan accepted my papers and gave me a long, heartfelt embrace as we parted in his office. The papers went speedily to Rome and through their full course of handling until the final approval by Pope Paul VI on July 15, 1968. The rescript of laicization was forwarded to the diocese where I was living at the time, and a sacramental marriage was arranged.

Jo Anne had come to the United States in late March 1968, greatly helped by Father John Daly's kindly assistance on passport and visa matters. We two then began our long wait together for the permission to marry in the Church. The daily mail was a daily trial as weeks rolled into months. How many weekdays and Sundays we went to Mass and Holy Communion together, begging God to hear our prayers and speedily unite us through His Church.

A few close friends came to our rescue during those five weary months of waiting. The Jesuits were now far away and the whole process was out of their hands anyway. However, one close Jesuit friend in Rome was highly instrumental in keeping me sane and informed of the process as it went along. All he asked was my trust in God and trust in the Church that it would handle these matters as expeditiously as possible, considering the load of such cases as mine coming in of late.

My family and many relatives were also far away and could not keep up with these involved, revolutionary, modern Church movements. They were told by their priest friends that I would never get the permission. The understanding friends that kept us alive literally and spiritually stuck close, encouraging Jo Anne and me to continue in our mutual love and to continue in our love of God and the Church. They saw no incompatibility in all these loves. I can never forget their deep effect on our lives.

The day of the wedding was set, and after the usual marriage license and blood tests, the arrangements for a quiet ceremony in a private chapel were completed. At the wedding Mass on August 30, 1968, Jo Anne and I proudly held each other's hands and before the priest and two witnesses promised union until death. From that God-planned union there is no release and no request to leave it behind and form another such union. No, this great sacrament of marriage flooded us with graces as we calmly spoke the words of contract: "I do," and "I take."

At the Communion time of the Nuptial Mass, I was startled to see the chalice of the Precious Blood being offered to us along with Christ's Body in the Host. I knew this could be done at weddings, but I had forgotten about it at my own wedding and had not specifically requested it. Happily I sipped the saving Blood of Christ, even though I did not consecrate it as I had done exactly 5,303 times before I had left the priesthood. But now to share this heavenly food with my wife was a pleasure unexplainable to one who is just a priest or just a newly married man. Only the laicized priest knows the glory of that moment. It was more important for me to receive than to consecrate.

What a blessing it is to be down on the human level again. I feel more secure of my eternity as a noncelibate layman than I did as a celibate priest. I will serve my God and my Church as an ordinary layman and seek heaven by ordinary paths. No more for me is the lofty but lonely pedestal of the priesthood as it exists today. I want and need the warm, human love of a woman as my wife to help me live a better life on earth and to help me reach heaven. I thank God for her and for the permission granted to me by the Church to have her as my proper wife in the eyes of God and men.

3

I APPEALED TO GOD

by D. Terence Netter

D. Terence Netter was born April 12, 1929, in New Rochelle, New York. He attended Georgetown Prep School and entered the Society of Jesus in 1947 at the age of eighteen. His training took him from Wernersville, Pennsylvania, to Woodstock, Maryland, and later to Bellarmine College, Plattsburgh, New York, where he received his B.A. in 1953 and his M.A. in 1954. As a Jesuit scholastic he taught mathematics and Latin in high school, and philosophy in college, before beginning his theological studies in 1957 at Innsbruck, Austria, where he was ordained in 1960.

After two more years of study abroad he returned to this country in 1962. He received his master of fine arts degree from George Washington University in 1965 and, in June of the same year, held his first one-man art exhibit in New York. He then continued to teach aesthetics and art, first at Georgetown and later at Fordham. He resigned from Fordham in June 1965 because of his announced intention to marry Therese Franzese.

After his petition for the necessary dispensation to Rome went unanswered for eight months, he and Miss Franzese were married in a civil ceremony. From 1962 to 1968 he preached almost every Sunday, first at Holy Trinity Church in Georgetown and then at Most Holy Trinity Church, East Hampton, Long Island, where he spent his summers. He still considers that he is practicing his ministry informally in his painting and his dealings with his numerous students. Having had two one-man art exhibits in 1968, one in Falmouth, Massachusetts, and one in New York, he is presently self-employed in the loft in Greenwich Village where he lives and works.

In 1965, when I was at Georgetown, an article appeared in *The New York Times* about the possibility of a change in the Church's policy on celibacy. My father had read the article and told me about it on the telephone. He wanted to know if this would affect me. I remember saying to him jocularly: "Don't worry, Pop, I have enough problems without marriage!"

I should not have said that because he took my reply as a permanent decision. One lives as a child of his times, and I was living in a time when optional celibacy was a distinct *possibility*. I had therefore no way of knowing that it would not be a possibility *for me*.

I knew, of course, that priests are allowed to marry in the Eastern Catholic Churches, and I had long been intellectually convinced that celibacy should be made optional so that the People of God, especially in poor countries, such as those of South America, might get the service they need so badly. When one is convinced of something on principle, that conviction opens up doors that might otherwise appear to be locked forever.

I had never planned to marry, and when I took my vow, I meant it. A lot has happened to me in the three years since I made that statement to my father. A lot happens to anyone in three years. There was a certain difference of opinion on academic matters with some members of the administration at Georgetown, which occasioned my accepting a better offer from Fordham. For a reason still unknown to me, however, I was not allowed to come to Fordham immediately, even though the position was waiting for me.

I spent one whole summer, the summer of 1966, betwixt and between. I shall never forget that summer. I spent it painting and preaching in East Hampton, a watering place for artists and intellectuals and socialites on the tip of Long Island.

On the surface things were idyllic: a great barn to paint in across the street from where the great Jackson Pollock used to paint and down the street from de Kooning's house; lots of friends; a remarkably enthusiastic response from the parishioners to a series of sermons I preached on "The Cosmic Christ"; sun, sand, surf, and the beautiful scenery of the Hamptons.

But inside I was in anguish. I was living under a ban, later lifted, which I felt to be unjust. I was forced to rethink my commitment to obedience. Should one obey injustice? What is the proper relation of the individual vis-à-vis lawful authority? I had never had an authority problem before. I respected authority. I still do. But where does respect for authority leave off and cowardice begin?

I loved the Society of Jesus. I still do. Where do love and commitment to any society leave off, however, and where does the abdication of one's individuality and of one's personal mission begin? I was not mad at anybody and still am not. I knew that my opponents, whoever they were, were acting in good faith. But the instinct for self-preservation has a boiling point, even in the heart of a saint, which I do not claim to be. In short, my problem was with obedience, not celibacy.

Subsequently that mysterious ban was lifted, and I came to Fordham and took up my teaching post and all was forgiven. Things went on as usual. But inside I had changed. I no longer felt protected. I realized in a deeper way than ever before that one has not had the full Christian experience until one is persecuted by one's own.

This is not to say that I felt persecuted either by the Society of Jesus or by the institutional Church. I wish I could tell the world of the great kindness shown to me at Fordham in the two years before my marriage. Rather did I have an ever-increasing sense of personal mission; of being myself to be like Christ; of dying to that self in me that shunned the cross of loneliness and the vinegar of opposition.

I was not discontented with the order, any order, Jesuit or otherwise. I lean to the left on most issues. But this is probably as much from temperament as from anything else. I have long thought that conservatives are born, not made, that it is largely a matter of metabolism. I certainly do not resent, however, the existence of the conservatives.

Furthermore, by nature and nurture, I am something of an individualist, so that the community life-form of the order became increasingly less relevant to what I was doing—painting, which is, above all, a highly individualized enterprise. Yet I know priest-painters and nun-painters who thrive in their respective communities and as celibates, and so I do not want to generalize. In fact, I do not want to generalize at all, since my marriage was ultimately a personal statement, and I certainly did not enter into it in order to change the law of celibacy.

As I mentioned previously, I had long thought that celibacy should be made optional for priests in the West, but I did not marry to protest. I feel that the issue will be solved more by practical necessity than by anything else. I suppose, however, that even though I married to find positive values rather than to protest, my move was actually a protest and I must face up to that. This is why I finally agreed to be part of Father O'Brien's book.

After I married, I saw that my action had wider dimensions than the purely personal ones. My wife realizes this, too. So we have submitted to the publicity which ensued, feeling that the truth would be much less harmful than the surmises which always surround clandestine maneuvers. After all, marriage is a public as well as a private affair.

In any case, what happened during the school year of 1966-67 did not just happen. It happened in a certain climate of public opinion which was more and more acceptable to the notion of a married clergy, and it happened to me at a time when I was already in search for something—knowing not exactly what. I had always been a rather tortured person inside anyway. People say that they see it in my paintings. It would be surprising if it were not there.

I have always been convinced that my success as a preacher was due as much to the fact that I was always trying to overcome my own doubts as to anything else. Be that as it may, what happened was this. I saw from time to time that winter, always in the company of others, Therese Franzese, the sister of a former student of mine and a friend of one of my brothers. I also saw a lot of other people. The art world does not lack in communication, and university life is even more "groupy." Through a series of circumstances too complicated to relate, we realized separately and, strangely enough, on the same day that we were in love. So we did what was proper in the circumstances: we parted. This was in the spring of 1967.

Falling in love, of course, can happen to anyone, and no vow is proof against that. I do not know many priests who have not fallen in love at one time or another. In fact, I think it is one of the glories of the Catholic priesthood that most of the men in it are celibate by constant choice, not by lack of the inner power to love a woman. There are cases of escapism, I guess (where are there not?), but I have never met one, and I know many priests intimately.

Whatever one may judge of my subsequent decision to pursue that love in marriage, no thoughtful person can condemn me for having fallen in love. It happens to the best of us. My spiritual father knew this, of course, and when I recounted the event, he said: "The love is from God, but keep your horizons up." This I tried to do.

Therese, of course, was not just anybody. She lacked neither suitors nor intelligence, nor faith, nor means. She was twenty-five at the time; I was thirty-eight. Working at the Metropolitan Opera, she loved music as I loved art. We had much in common, including a great love for the Church and a desire to find Christ in other people more than anywhere else. Her family loved me and mine loved her.

But we parted. It would have been permanent if, after a few weeks, I had not asked her to see me again. It was during those few weeks in the spring of 1967 when I entered into the valley of decision. It was a valley from which I did not completely emerge until January 1, 1968. Then I sent my formal petition to Rome for the threefold permission one needs in such a case, namely: (1) to be released from one's vows (in my case the solemn vows of a professed Jesuit), (2) laicization, and (3) permission to marry.

Therese's position was this: Union with God was to be preferred to any other kind of union. But union with me could not be reconciled with union with God. Therefore the love had to be sacrificed for a greater love. And there is nothing wrong with that reasoning. It is, I suppose, as good a restatement as any of the law of Christ.

But I am of a more metaphysical bent. Why, I kept asking myself in those few weeks, could not union with God be achieved through our love? Had God ever said so? No: not in Scripture, nor in tradition. Though tradition had always held that celibacy, undertaken from the right motive, was a higher way of love, it had constantly affirmed that marriage was a sacrament.

But the Church said No, and the Church was considered, rightly or wrongly, the voice of God. The Church had not always said No, however, and does not say so today in the East where priests are allowed to marry. Could one say that only the celibate priests in Lebanon, for instance, could achieve union with God?

Why, then, would the consummation of our love in marriage exclude union with God, even though I was an ordained priest? I had committed myself. I had taken the vow. But would I have taken it if the alternative had been open to me? If the alternative were open to me now, I said to myself—that is, not between being a priest or not a priest (I have never doubted my vocation since ordination), but between being a celibate priest or a married priest—which would I choose?

Suppose the rule were changed in ten years, and I had lost my opportunity. What would happen to me inside? What good would I be? The question became far from simple to me and the answer was not forthcoming. Furthermore, I did not find inner peace during our separation. On the contrary, I felt insincere, hasty, and immature.

So I asked Therese to see me again, which she reluctantly consented to do. I described as well as I could the path which my reflections were leading me along and asked her to think it out herself. She began to have second thoughts. Well educated and clear thinking, she agreed to reconsider. It was tortuous for both of us. We consulted, only God knows, how many people, and still the path did not become clear. The storm within us did not so much throw us off course—since we were both of the mind that God's will was to be done—as to make each of us wonder if we might not head in another direction to find the appointed goal.

Suddenly it was summer. She was in New York, I in East Hampton. She wanted to go abroad for a month. I asked her not to do so, feeling that such a decision, if it ever came to a decision, should be mutual: whether to make the separation final or not. She consented. I guess I thought about nothing else till August. At that time I asked her to drive halfway out to meet me, for I had something to say.

What I said was in the form of a proposal. Since I could not make up my mind, I asked if she would wait a year. Then if I decided that I wanted to marry her before God and the hope for the eventual change of the Church's rule, I asked if she would do so. She said Yes. We both felt semipeaceful in this decision—more peaceful at any rate than during the past four months.

But one can live in the valley of decision for just so long. At the end of the summer I was back in New York, teaching and painting as usual. Externally things were orderly for both Therese and myself, but inside we were being torn apart. With any decision, however painful, one can live. With indecision something happens to all the psychological mechanisms. Hence we agreed to decide soon, rather than wait an entire year. So again we parted.

My studio at that time was on 95th Street, just off First Avenue. I used to walk along the river to clear my mind, to meditate, and simply to get fresh air. It was while walking by the river in September of 1967 that I came to my decision.

I searched my heart. I asked myself the question "If I give Therese up, why shall I do so?" On principle? But I was convinced that celibacy should be made optional. Because of my previous commitment? But it was a commitment made when the alternative was not possible. Furthermore, I knew that the mechanism existed in the Church to make the change legal.

Why, then? Friends had pointed out that the decision to marry in our circumstances would cause pain. But should a Christian let the fear of pain deter him from an appointed path? Others had pointed out that it would ruin my art career. But if success were dependent upon my position in the Church, would it not be false success anyway?

In short, after sifting through my motives, the only conscious motives I could find for giving up Therese were the fear of public opinion and loyalty to the Jesuits. But I had long since decided not to let fear determine my life, and I felt that those alone can help any group who wholeheartedly share the ideals of that group.

So there I was, knowing full well that human motivation is too complicated to be sifted out. I knew also how much room there is for self-deception in all life changes of such moment. I was aware also of what my resignation from the public ministry would mean to me and to my loved ones and to those who looked up to me. What was I to do?

Thus I was down to the elementary facts. I was faced not with an abstract choice between good and evil, but with a concrete one between what appeared to me to be two goods: either to continue to pursue my priestly vocation within the approved life-form of the Society of Jesus or to pursue it with Therese in a yet-to-be-approved way. I knew that I must seek approval from God, not men.

I was conscious that God would never approve of me if I were not true to myself. Finally I realized that I could no longer be true to myself within the life-form of the Jesuits, whose collective ideal is tremendous, but whose way of life I no longer felt capable of following. This was not because I lacked the moral strength to do so—my record stands for itself—but because I had the distinct conviction that God was calling me to travel another road.

How does a man know this? I do not know. I only know that grace is a constellation of circumstances and that the circumstance of my being in love with such a wonderful person at such a moment in history and at such a moment in my own life was no happenstance.

On that day, at a precise moment, walking along the East River on a rainy afternoon in September, I realized that asking Therese to marry me was the only authentic thing I could do. Otherwise for the rest of my life I would never be able to preach again, for personal authenticity was and is the heart of my message. Thus I made my decision, the hardest one I ever made. I felt purified and at peace. That peace has never left me in spite of the pain which inevitably followed.

Therese accepted my proposal. It was then that I decided to resign from the ministry only because we both wanted to remain within the Church. So I come to the point of the story where I answer the question: Why did I resign from the ministry? I did so because it is the only thing one can do at this moment in history if one is a priest and wants to marry within the Church.

Otherwise I would not have resigned, for I am a priest and still want to minister to the People of God as a priest. I look forward to the day when I can resume my public ministry. I hope this book hastens that day. So does my wife. Otherwise I would not be part of it, because we derive no pleasure from public exposure.

In January 1968 I petitioned the Vatican for release from my vow of celibacy. For eight long, interminable, suspense-ridden months I waited. But no answer came and perhaps none would ever come. Surely I had given the authorities more than ample time. No just or fair tribunal could ask one to wait longer.

I then realized that with a good conscience, I must transfer my appeal from the inactive, silent, and functionless tribunal of Rome to the tribunal of God. The Vatican had failed to use the mechanism specifically established to transmit such a release, which it has done with increasing frequency in recent years.

So we turned to God with the sure confidence that He who reads the secrets of all hearts would read ours and would not fail to see that marriage without the witness of a priest was not something we were undergoing out of contempt for the law, but rather because there was lacking due process of the law in our case. So on July 11, 1968, Therese and I were married at City Hall in New York. We married with peace in our hearts. Afterward we attended Mass. We could wait no longer because the suspense was beginning to erode our relationship.

We are still waiting to hear from Rome as I write this. When we do, we will have our marriage blessed by the Church. Technically excommunicated at the moment I do not, however, feel existentially excommunicated. We have certain clerical friends who give us Communion, although we will not receive from one who does not know the case. Still we long for full reinstatement, for we belong in the community of the faithful. Our faith has never been stronger and we have no bitterness in our hearts, only a certain amazement at the cruelty (unintended, I am sure) involved in such useless delaying tactics.

Why were we not given permission to marry, even though we went through existing channels with rigorous adherence to protocol? Probably because they have not yet had time to process the case in Rome. When there are at least 600 million Roman Catholics in the world, is there any reason why such a case could not be handled by the local bishop or archbishop? Everyone on this side of the ocean has been so kind, so willing to help, including the officials in the diocesan court. But from the other side—nothing.

But why should we complain? Ours is but one small example of the Church's failing to meet the needs of the times. The Church is, of course, conservative by nature: it is in existence to preserve the two-thousand-year-old tradition of Christ. But why cannot the tradition remain even while new ways and means are sought to find new structures adapted to meet new needs? What is needed is a switch from the either/or attitude to the both/and attitude. The conservatism of the Catholic Church is only one side of it. There have always been liberals also. Unfortunately, until recently the conservative side has been taken by the world to be the only side, and it presents such a joyless face; it appears always to be so threatened. But threatened by what? Certainly not by such as I.

The Church is indeed threatened, but not by those who want optional celibacy or more room for freedom of conscience in such an obviously doubtful moral issue as birth control or more voice in Church affairs. The Church is threatened rather by disinterest, by the widespread defection of the youth, and by the dismal prophets of doom in high places who regard any movement which originates in the ranks as subversive.

People do not leave the Church anymore: they are just suddenly not present. The "youth of today" are no better or worse than the youth of any other day. What they are seeking is what we all seek: a communion of love. And when they do not find this in the Church, they turn to other things. Those who seek for change should be of no major concern to the Church until they stop concerning themselves with the Church.

What rule was ever changed in the Church or in any other society except through the initiative of individuals? And that is all that mandatory celibacy for priests in the West is: a rule, which could be changed by a fiat, like fish on Friday. The Church is the living Body of Christ, not a chess game played by theologians, much less a totalitarian state in which all reform originates from above. And in living organisms change takes place through practical necessity, not through speculation. The issue of optional celibacy accordingly is quite clearly not in the realm of theological speculation at all. It is a question of giving priority either to a mere custom which once had meaning or to the need of the Church for priests in a world in which the celibate elite are not and never will be numerous enough to serve the needs of the people.

So I resigned from the ministry because I had no recourse if I wanted to stay within the Church of my belief, and also because I want the ministry to be larger and more effective, including others like myself who are perfectly willing to serve in a lesser role. I love the Church as well as my wife and I want it to grow and prosper.

I know ten young men of superb qualifications who would enter the ministry tomorrow if they knew they would one day have the option to marry. Not every one of them would. But they want the option. So the issue is one of freedom more than celibacy. And is this not the real issue which confronts the Church as a whole?

Why will the Church not leave this up to the individual? Not every priest should marry. Not every priest even wants to. But what is the shock all about? Are we not dealing merely with a custom which has come to be so accepted as to have the force of law not only on the books but in the conscience of those who have the power to abrogate the rule?

What is really shocking is not the growing numbers of priests who marry but the shock itself, for it reveals bad education and the failure of the masses to be able to distinguish between the law of God and the law of men, between the substantial and accidental, between the real problems which confront a Christian today, such as war, mass starvation, social injustice, and the rules of the game.

In a sense it is a shame that such a book as this must be written. But theory must yield to fact, and the fact is that public opinion must be prepared to accept a married clergy before the hierarchy will begin to act. I hope my contribution will speed that day, for I look forward, as I am sure most married priests do, to the day when I can resume my public ministry. Meanwhile I am content to practice my priesthood in less formal ways—through my painting, through dealing with students, and by preaching Christ's message of love in private. And I often think of the words in Milton's sonnet on his blindness: "They also serve who only stand and wait."

4

I'M NOT LONELY NOW

by Arthur F. Le Blanc

Arthur F. Le Blanc was born on January 13, 1926, in Lynn, Massachusetts. He and his only brother survived the Depression through the efforts of their mother's occupation of hairdressing. After graduating from St. John's Preparatory School, Danvers, Massachusetts, he spent 1944–45 in the U.S. Army Air Corps. After returning to civil life, he studied at Norwich University, Northfield, Vermont, receiving his B.A. degree in 1948.

Although awarded a fellowship leading to the Ph.D. degree at the University of Notre Dame, Arthur Le Blanc decided to teach for a year, while thinking about a vocation to the priesthood. He took the necessary Latin and taught at St. Michael's College in Winooski, Vermont. From 1949 to 1956 he attended St. Paul's College, Washington, D.C., where he received his M.A. degree. After his ordination as a Paulist priest in 1956, he served as chaplain to the Catholic students at Tufts Medical School, Massachusetts Institute of Technology, Brandeis University, and Babson Institute from 1956 to 1960.

In 1966 he received his Ph.D. in developmental and clinical psychology from Ohio State University, where he

served as chaplain to the Catholic students. He was clinical
psychologist and research director at the American Foundation of Religion and Psychiatry in New York. On February 1, 1968, he resigned from the Paulist community
and married Helen Marie Haggerty. He is now a psychologist at the Camarillo State Hospital in southern California.

The old saying about being lonely in a crowd is really true, and it can
be just as true for a priest in a religious order as for anyone else. It
was certainly so in my case, and I do not hesitate to name loneliness
as the prime reason for my leaving the Paulists and the religious life.

One's fellows in a religious order are not supposed to be a "crowd,"
though; they are supposed to be a family, sharing one another's joys
and griefs, successes and failures. But in the course of the twelve years
following ordination, I did not find this familial sharing. It was a
group of individuals, each with his own work, interests, and outside
friends.

My work and interests were of little or no consequence to the others.
When I came "home" after a tour of several days, it was common to
hear: "Oh, were you away?" My presence or absence was not noticed
—*I* was not noticed.

Well, I did not join the Paulists for this nonconcern. Initially, I had
rejected the idea of the diocesan priesthood for me basically out of
fear of being alone. I knew away back in 1949 that companionship was
essential for my well being. As it turned out in the late 1950s and in
the 1960s, I became vividly aware that I had become terrified and alone
in my religious "home." Riding home on the crowded subway, I began
to wonder who would be sitting with me at the evening meal. Would
they understand that I didn't care about new surplices for the altar
boys or the decrease in collections or the Holy Name speaker?

My daily concern for the mentally ill in a large outpatient clinic was
a far cry from the parish demands or the missionary stories or the out-
put of the press. Such heterogeneity of interests prevented a meaningful exchange. Meanwhile, lunchtime had been filled with excitement

and pleasure, stimulation and concern from fellow mental-health professionals. Lunchtime meant an opportunity to express joy and success, the degree of depression and elation.

The religious house was forced, tiring, and banefully repetitious. I laugh when I think of the many times that the reader at meditation time read from Thomas a Kempis. "The more you go among men, the less a man you become." I found that the more I went among my fellow professionals at the clinic, the more human I became. I guess that a Kempis and I have a different definition of a man.

And so I looked forward to escaping from the surface living of the religious house to the real world of work, specifically my teaching and psychotherapy. I even took from patients who needed (and had) my interest and support perhaps only slightly more than I needed theirs. It is rather telling that one can feel more given to and giving with professional clients than with one's fellow religious.

So as I say, the enrichment of my emotional life came from outside the religious community. But having taken from my good friends in the laity, I was the more frustrated, as I was unable to repay their kindnesses adequately. Remember, it was forbidden to entertain friends in my own "home." I was reminded that they belonged to the laity.

Many people say, I know, that priests and religious have a long time to think about the consequences of the once seemingly final step. For a veteran of World War II and a college graduate, from 1949 to 1956 is a long time. But one thinks in terms of past and present experiences. In psychology, we speak of building up "expectancies." The army, college, and the seminary each yielded a community spirit. In turn, the seminary promised further fellowship and emotional nourishment in the active priesthood.

Why this spirit would decline so sharply in the rectories is a baffler. It can't be totally attributable to advancing years. If some way could be found to retain the spirit of the training years, I am sure the members would be happier, and fewer would leave. But if one counts on and expects such an atmosphere, as I did, he will be the harder hit by the ecclesiastical banalities.

There will always be the problem of celibacy. I have no doubt that many men can find in an open, mature, and loving religious community all the support that they need to lead useful and rewarding lives. Some, however, will find that they require the attention and devotion found only in the marital state. Whether I could have considered marriage had I experienced that kind of religious life that I deeply desired is an open question. Probably not, for most studies in social psychology indicate that if one's needs for affection, respect, and recognition are being met in one's current life pattern, he will not normally forsake this for a different style of life where fulfillment of these needs is problematical.

However, forced as I was to seek support and love outside my religious community, one person gradually became the center of my interest. Prior to my marriage in February of 1968, at social gatherings I had always felt like a fifth wheel. Couples came and left together; I came and left alone. Or, I came with a couple to make real the phrase "Three's a crowd." The lonely trips "home" and the frightened nature of the home to which I returned contrasted sharply with the companionship and lack of fear that I saw in others. Yes, at forty-two years of age, I was lonely and fearful. After all, paternalism breeds fear.

While doing my clinical internship in psychology, I was fortunate enough to work on a large research project sponsored by the United States Government. My part in the endeavor was to attempt to teach a twelve-year-old boy to speak for the first time in his life. For seven months, I worked two hours a day feeding him pieces of candy, holding brightly colored paper before his eyes, and vocalizing words. Like a miniature Helen Keller story, he finally burst forth with "M-M-Mother." Two hours later, it was a clear "Mother" and "walk."

He loved to be taken out of the hospital for a walk through the local stores. We did this on two lunch hours a week. Needless to say, I and the entire team of psychiatrists, psychologists, speech therapists, nurses, and technicians were delighted that March day of 1963. I virtually flew home to the rectory to blurt out at the evening meal: "Tommy said some words."

My excited announcement was greeted with: "How old is Tommy?" When I explained that he was twelve, the conversation moved on as one remarked: "What's so big deal about that?" My cries of "first words" were drowned out by some missionary's caricature of a recent pastor.

I ate and anxiously waited to find the laity who would listen and understand and celebrate the "good news" that a twelve-year-old boy had spoken and therefore might speak even more. It was just one month later that the cardinal of Los Angeles discovered that a priest with a scientific hat was in his archdiocese.

My second major reason for leaving was what I could only see as an unconscionable waste of my talent and education. From 1954 through 1966, I had graduate courses and clinical experience in the area of psychotherapy in six universities and two training hospitals. One could say that I had acquired some special skills. My religious community, however, had no place for these skills. Psychology was not to be part of the seminary training.

The rector was fearful that such knowledge would promote introspective thinking. My gosh, we couldn't have any of that. What would the neighbors say? So, there was no place for my teaching skills within my order. State universities, Catholic colleges, and medical schools would allow me in the classrooms and at the lecture podium, but my own religious family had no room in the academic "inn."

Too much effort, tears, and anxiety had gone into psychology for me to leave it on the shelf. The populace was, and is, crying for the alleviation of mental suffering. Being a fifth wheel among missionaries and parish priests, I found a home in an interdenominational psychiatric training center. There, at the American Foundation of Religion and Psychiatry, I could teach priests, ministers, and rabbis psychotherapy. There at the foundation, the study of behavior was not feared. It was welcomed. Meanwhile, my religious community seemed pleased that I was placed, especially with such a salary. The following episode should give an idea of what this paying position meant to my fellow religious.

While walking out of the front door of the rectory one day to get a haircut, I encountered the local superior and one of the order's consultors. The latter said to the local superior, "What is he doing, leaving the rectory in a sweater?" To which the latter replied, "For the amount of money he brings into this house, he can wear anything." It is difficult for me to be wanted for my salary.

Again, I found an immense divergence from the days of the seminary with its training principles. As I said previously, the seminary promised meaningful fellowship in the priesthood. It didn't come! Likewise, the seminary spoke of God's will and direction from superiors. So, in my work-world I was violating, or not finding, the second expectancy. My petitioning the professional world for a "job" was a long way from going the route of the superior's will. With time, I found myself making plans not simply for the next academic year but for the next five years. Plans were envisioned, research proposed, new training imagined. Yet how can a professional person plan when he doesn't even know where he'll be living next year? Like a black cloud hung the possibility of transfer.

The loneliness and unuse of professional skill are the data, the facts, the perceptions, the feelings. I'd like to pause and see if such can be eliminated for those religious who remain in the diverse orders.

It seems that loneliness mushrooms in large rectories. Mere numbers reduce the possibility of meaningful communication. Façade becomes a necessary defense mechanism when our expectancies are not firm. How can we make accurate interpersonal expectancies when we don't even know who will be home? No wonder lots of behavioral scientists refer to the schizoid quality of communication within religious houses. It is the plexiglass stance with laughter, joking, kidding, and meaningless chatter bouncing off our defensive armor.

I want the reader to know that I did have two wonderful, meaningful years. There were three of us. Those years had tears, disappointment, anxiety, joy, and success. There was, moreover, no loneliness and no fear. Lack of distance destroyed the possibility of loneliness, and lack of paternalism eliminated the seeds of fear. As to the issue of no use of skills, I recall a mild lecture from my hometown pastor.

"Father," he said, "don't let me hear of you teaching our local seminarians about psychotherapy, existentialism, or those guys Sartre and Camus. I want young priests to say Mass, hear confessions, and train altar boys."

Well, that was a long time ago—1967. Possibly, the future will be different. The wearing of two hats, priest and scientist, will not be held suspect. With the dissolution of the parish structure and attention given to the individual needs of our diversely educated people, a specialized ministry may find its way onto the American scene. Those courageous and dedicated priests of the racial and poverty apostolate have pierced the old cycle that demanded traditional role-playing.

Until the 1950s, the priest was limited to Roman collars, French cuffs, days on duty, sick calls, and a virtual waiting for the heavenly reward. I feel that we are to see more of the worker-priest. It is one of the mature means of reducing paternalism and alleviating fear. It enables a full-blooded American an opportunity to achieve; my age group and the one below me have been taught to be achievers. I am therefore more hopeful that skills will be used than I am that loneliness will be reduced.

My own loneliness has ceased. My skills are being used in the real world of here and now. I can unlock my front door with the expectancy of seeing my wife. I can in fact bring home the laity as well as the clergy. There is no paternalistic figure demanding that we eat at this moment. The end of the evening news does not mean a long trek to a bare room. Of course, the work-world is tiring; the bills are depressing; taxes are coming; and my clothes carry a notice "On sale," but it is for real.

From what I've said so far one might get the impression that all my reasons for leaving concerned my relations with other members of the religious order. This is not true.

My few priestly activities, that is "priestly" as defined by the organized Church, became rather meaningless. After two days in the confessional box during the Christmas rush of 1965, I suddenly realized that I hadn't heard any material that I could label as sinful. Staying in the box was simply supplying the means of promoting a neurotic method of handling this false guilt. From that time I would hear the sins of anyone who sought me out. My office became the new box. If they asked for the anonymity of the darkened box, it was equally okay with me, but I fled from the usual hours which support neurosis.

Putting oil on a dead person's head began to look awfully stupid. Bringing the Eucharist to the aged is laudable. But awaking the senile at 6:30 A.M. for a wafer that used to mean the presence of Christ back in their lucid days doesn't seem to be my way of starting my daily priestly duties. In terms of Mass, my years on a university campus were filled to the point where the "cup runneth over."

From these creative experiences, I moved to a basement church in New York City. It wasn't my church, it was en route to work. I remember well that for the last two years I looked out to the congregation of two. There they were—two elderly ladies speaking to God in their foreign tongues, while I performed my liturgy. If I didn't get sent to this performance, I knew that the absentee pastor had enough of Florida.

As for preaching, the opportunity was in the Newman apostolate and I feel that I used the moments well. After all, the Newman circle has been a church within the Church for years. Our Catholic world was so different from their eventual parish that I questioned the practical wisdom of our good intentions. It is so horrible to build false expectations.

There in the Newman world, post-Conciliar thoughts were verbalized in pre-Conciliar times. When I attempted to bring the new news to the parishes, pastors complained to my superiors and bishops finally heard that the living word was being spoken outside of the far-out, liberal, kooky university walls. For the last two years of my priestly garb, I had to sit listening to the good news being spread in the old irrelevant way.

So much for my priestly activities as such. Let us move to my final area of discouragement—the hierarchy.

How would you like to come home to a factory-working parent who was proud of his son's priesthood, only to tell him that his number-one son had been expelled from a diocese by none other than a cardinal? They just don't prepare you for these things in the seminary.

My first encounter with the hierarchy since the day of ordination took the form of swift removal from a diocese. Without giving me an interview, without personally phoning or writing to me, I was notified through the pastor that the land of Los Angeles, California, would have no priests who also wore the hat of psychology. There was no interview, no court of appeals, no review board, simply a plane ticket. That was a tearful ride east.

At present, I teach psychiatric residents how to terminate a therapeutic relationship slowly and prudently. The cardinal of Los Angeles had obviously never heard of the fundamentals of psychotherapy. My sudden departure violated every concept in the ethics of therapy. My superior general pleaded from across the country; I begged for an interview. All we heard was: Go, Priest, Go!

My second hierarchial experience came from across the Atlantic. From Los Angeles to Rome seems distant on a child's globe, but it is a stone's throw in the world of chancery communication.

In December of 1965 I presented psychological research on the issue of whom we usually tell terrible things about ourselves. In psychological circles this is called "self-disclosure." As a repercussion of this liturgical conference, the Catholic press publicized my suggestion that we should find diverse means of confessing sins. I was in no way asking for the elimination of the current confessional box for those penitents who could and wanted to use it. I was, however, asking for ways and means appropriate for those who could not and would not use the conventional box.

From across the Atlantic came a Latin manuscript warning me to keep my nose out of the sacrament of penance. At that particular time, I was too busy with other research to carry on an erratic dispute with Rome. Furthermore, I couldn't read their Latin and they couldn't read my statistical language.

Some twelve months later, I returned to the confessional issue. My other research was finished and the earlier publicity in the Catholic press had brought numerous letters of appeal, begging me to continue my efforts to obtain diverse confessional settings. People with a need and desire to tell God of their sorrow for their sins were pleading and continue to plead for a variety of "approved" means. The psychological needs of people are just too diverse to demand that everyone adjust to the one way—the darkened box.

Reopening of the confessional topic brought scorn and denouncement from local bishops. Missionaries felt threatened and bombarded the Catholic press with articles disclaiming the right of a behavioral scientist to look at this "holy sacrament of Christ."

As you can readily see, it was once again the same public sin on my part. "Thou shalt not wear two hats!" Strange, I had thought that the Church would be pleased with my efforts to acquire another hat, that of a scientist, especially in the age of science. Like a lamb among wolves, I naïvely came with the experience of having heard confessions, with the sociological view of the development of a Catholic, with ten years of training in the study of behavior. I was too frightening, little me; so again I was silenced.

In psychiatry we call this fear of looking "telescopic vision." It usually results from anxiety that has been generated by some outside source. For the American bishops, I was an outside source asking them to look at the needs of many Catholics who cannot or will not use the darkened confessional box. I was told to stop looking to the right or left. It had to be the box, or "Go, Priest! Go!"

So I went back to wearing one hat in my psychotherapy clinic. I went there to teach people to look to the right and to the left and not to be frightened by what they see. What's out there can't hurt you. You can only hurt yourself.

It was when I realized that staying in the religious order meant hurting myself that I left. One is really hurting when at forty-two years of age he is lonely, frightened, and unable to use his skills. It is sad to say that many others must stay with their loneliness and fear because their one hat, the priestly biretta, is not economically negotiable. Without my other hat, my scientific degrees, and experience, it would have been another world for me. I only know my world.

In mid-January of 1968 I was having lunch with the faculty of our junior seminary. Across the table sat a classmate of mine. I sat with my forty-two years and two days and he with his thirty-nine years and some months.

"Art," he said, "how can these men our age ever think of getting married? I'm already looking forward to retirement from this teaching job and basking in the sun of California. Who wants bills, children, and such responsibility at our age?"

Thank God, the conversation turned into frivolity about aging. How could I tell him and the ten fellow religious that this was my last trip to the seminary, my last meal with them in this environment? After all, Helen and I had just secured our marriage license the previous day. We were anxiously waiting for Friday afternoon, February 2.

A few close priest friends, whom we had told in advance, had volunteered to marry us. News of these events moves swifter, however, than the estimate of casualties in Vietnam. In fact, we refused to allow these priests and our Catholic friends to the eventual ceremony. But both clergy and laity insisted. So we kept date and place between us, our minister, and our non-Catholic friends. We thought we did! The age of fearing ecclesiastical retribution is over. Friendship cuts across the barriers of medieval controls.

We partially wished they didn't find us, for it was the most horrible, foggy, rainy day that I've ever experienced in Newark, New Jersey. They came into a beautiful red brick Lutheran church to participate in a liturgy that I helped to write. One of my students at the American Foundation of Religion and Psychiatry was the pastor of this church and a Church of Christ minister. We stood before a statue of the

Sacred Heart in a high-ceilinged sanctuary to promise before God that we would go where the other would go.

As an officiating priest, I had stood many times with my back to the altar and book in hand. It was a rather moving moment to stand facing the altar and the statue of the Sacred Heart with Helen in hand. The bridesmaid and female guests cried. The male guests looked at their wet feet and probably thought of fighting their way through the 5 P.M. traffic to the reception.

Every wedding has its little moments of remembrance: the flower girl drops the bouquet, an usher puts his big foot through a lace train and the bridegroom drops the ring. Well, we had to have ours, only ours turned out to be beautiful.

Unknown to Helen, it was to be a double-ring ceremony. Thanks to a friend, we got a buy in the jewelry market on the Lower East Side of New York City. The price for her wedding band was so reduced that I sneaked back two days later to get a matching band. We both wanted such, but we were too broke. So during the ceremony, when the minister asked her, "And what will you give?" she responded without flinching, "All I have is my love."

She turned red with surprise, pleasure, and delight as her bridesmaid handed her a wedding band while whispering: "And you also have a wedding ring to give as a sign of your love." Needless to say, I eventually heard in the quiet hours of the night: "Why didn't you tell me about the other ring? I was so embarrassed." She may have been momentarily embarrassed, but I am still hearing those spontaneous words whispered amid the patter of the Newark rain: "All I have is my love."

I suppose that Catholic readers are inquisitive about such notions as dispensations, marriage before a priest, and validation. Honestly, these terms have lost their meaning. It seems outlandish to attempt to present my feelings on a sheet of paper for the perusal of some unknown Italian cardinal. He doesn't even know how tall or fat I am, whether I sleep well or not, let alone the multifarious reasons that prompted me to think about marriage at the age of forty-two.

Anyhow, a rainy Friday in February meant the setting for a good behavior, the marriage of Helen and Arthur. Each Sunday and sometimes on other days, we come before another statue of the Sacred Heart to receive of the Eucharist as a sign of our communion with one another and in turn our communion with the historical Christ. If one of us decides that it isn't the time to communicate through the Eucharist, neither of us does. Communion in that church for us is ourselves. Getting back to that Friday in February, it's said that rain on one's wedding day is a lucky sign.

Now, it isn't lonely. I don't feel frightened and I'm exercising my skills some fifty hours a week. It will be a fifty-hour week for a long time. After all, 1969 will be my first encounter with an income tax form, and I hear that I "can't charge it!"

Why don't you call me after April? I won't be lonely, for we two shall be three. I might be frightened, but it won't be from paternalism. I shall still be using my scientific hat on my forty autistic children. As yet, it is difficult for them just to look straight ahead, let alone to the right or left. If you pray with me, as I do each time during the Eucharistic meal, these little ones will decrease their "telescopic vision." After all, there is always hope with children.

5

NOT REALLY LEAVING

by Robert M. Duggan

Robert M. Duggan was born in New York City on November 23, 1939. He entered St. Joseph's Seminary, Dunwoodie, New York, where he received a B.A. in philosophy in 1960 and an M.A. in moral theology in 1964. Ordained in May 1964, he served as an assistant pastor at St. Ann's parish in Manhattan which includes part of Greenwich Village, the Bowery, and lower Fifth Avenue, an area in which many Spanish-speaking people live.

He studied Spanish and intercultural relations for two summers at the Catholic University of Puerto Rico. In September 1965 he went to Rome where he studied canon law at Lateran University for fifteen months. He concentrated on parish structure and the meaning of the Christian community. He traveled to many countries of Europe, including the Soviet Union. In December 1966 while on a visit to New York, he was reassigned by Cardinal Spellman to St. Barnabas parish in the Bronx.

On November 1, 1967, he submitted a letter of resignation and a request for laicization to His Eminence and was granted an immediate leave of absence. In December he was appointed by the board of directors of the Na-

tional Association for Pastoral Renewal as national coordinator. In June 1968 he married Dianne Connelly of
South Colton, New York. At present he is studying for a
master's degree in human relations at New York University.

Discussing why I left the priesthood makes it important to describe
what I left. In a letter to friends and relatives announcing my resignation I wrote: "I have reached a decision that I can better contribute to
the work of bringing the good news of Christ to the world as a layman
than as a member of the clergy. I still feel very deeply the call of the
Spirit that brought me to ordination, but I can no longer correlate that
call with my life as a member of the clergy."

Preparing a thesis in Rome two years earlier I discovered that to
seriously discuss how a parish might become the Christian Community
described by Vatican II, modern theology, and the Acts of the Apostles,
it would be necessary to discuss clerical celibacy. I was told that this
was impossible. Celibacy was a "given" part of Church structure.

A few months after coming to that impasse, I met Dianne Connelly
on a Day of Recollection. During the discussions she asked me to explain what celibacy meant to me. The more I tried to make sense, the
less sure I was that what I was saying made sense to me. A few weeks
later at another discussion, Dianne said: "I wonder what it would be
like if you weren't a priest." I was shocked. No one had ever said that
to me. I knew I was having similar feelings, but I wouldn't dare express
them.

This recalled a letter I had written several months earlier in response
to some questions about changes going on in the Church. Regarding
celibacy I wrote: "That is something that will have to change eventually
(I would hate to be one of the people involved in trying to change it—
it will be murder!)" I still remember stopping after typing that line and
thinking to myself: "Duggan, don't be so glib. You will be sorry you
wrote that so easily."

I could remember two years before ordination making a private retreat to think about accepting subdeaconate and the obligation of celibacy. I went to a cottage on Greenwood Lake near New York City with

a stack of books and my bathing suit. For a full week I read and argued with myself. The decision I made is still clear to me. I wanted to be a priest, to be of service to people. I had no desire to be celibate. In fact, I suffered a great deal that week because I knew I was very much attracted to marriage. However, I would accept celibacy as a condition of ordination to the priesthood.

My desire in becoming a priest was precisely to serve people. I wanted to do the things done by the priests in the parish where I had grown up. They were much in demand and provided important service to people in the neighborhood. At least it seemed important to me at the time. Although I would not have used the terms then, I looked on the Church and priesthood as vehicles for accomplishing certain things in the world. When I discovered a few years later that the clerical way of life and celibacy were obstacles, rather than helps, to that, there was really no other option than to resign.

In many ways the seminary prepared me for a world that hardly existed by the time of my ordination. It was dying as fast as second-generation Irish were moving to suburbia. The experiences that washed over me in the first months after ordination, especially at St. Ann's parish on East Twelfth Street in Manhattan, created questions that started me on the process that put me where I am today and opened me to continuous change in the future.

Perhaps those questions would not have had the same impact on my life had I not been given the opportunity to study in Rome. There I discovered modern theology. For the first time I read philosophy which showed me other ways of understanding life than that of the scholastic philosophical formulas which we memorized in first philosophy at Saint Joseph's Seminary.

The experience of a new philosophical approach was the most important factor in opening my mind. Problems raised by my parish experience were nonproblems in the scholastic system. But when I could look at the world as a series of relationships, rather than as a system of fixed absolutes, those problems could become very real. Most importantly they became something I could work with and attempt to solve.

Even with that opportunity to study, I doubt that I would have had the courage to express my convictions were it not for several other experiences: a trip I made to the Soviet Union, a friendship with a dynamic priest from Florence, a struggle shared with some American priests in Rome in trying to express an opinion to our bishops, and most importantly the challenge of loving Dianne.

I met Dianne in April of 1966. She left Rome on June 1. We were to meet again in Paris at the end of June. I spent the intervening weeks trying to develop a clearer understanding of what was going on inside of me. Dianne was lively, beautiful, and intellectually stimulating. She had a powerful emotional effect on me. It was hard and yet so important to do some clear thinking. I knew that the law of celibacy had to change. I knew also that I was not a celibate by charism of the Holy Spirit. I tried again to look at celibacy as something valuable in order to accomplish something else.

However, I became frightened. As I struggled to reject my feelings for Dianne, the first things that came to mind were not high motives of service and dedication. Rather, I found myself afraid that I might not be able to love one person. I realized that until this point I had always been able to draw a line in every relationship; never had I committed myself to loving one person. Suddenly, I became aware that I had the fantastic security of a home and food plus $150 a month provided by the diocese; perhaps I couldn't make a living. I was afraid of rejection by family and friends. I was unsure of my sexual adequacy. These were the factors that asked me to reject Dianne. Strangely, in spite of all I had said about not wanting honors, the fact that I would never be an important person in the diocese now proved a significant reality.

This reaction shook me to my roots. I began to wonder if I had accepted celibacy to achieve higher goals or to avoid hard realities. The fact that these were spontaneous reactions probably did more to keep alive my relationship with Dianne than any other factor. I was really upset to discover that my value system had roots very different from what I had expected.

When Dianne and I met again in Paris, the uppermost thing in my mind was to avoid involving her in a difficult situation such as any consideration of marriage would certainly be. At first I wouldn't even mention that the idea had entered my mind. Finally, I showed her a letter I had written to a cousin but had never mailed. In it I said, "I have met the girl I would marry if I could marry." I remember we sat together later that day by the Seine dreaming of what it would be like if we were free to marry. It seemed so impossible!

I wouldn't kiss Dianne. I wanted to very much, but I knew that I had to work out our relationship on the intellectual level. To have expressed the emotional reactions that were pent up inside would have destroyed for me the possibility of working out an adequate understanding of this experience in terms of past experience and values.

We spent about a week together. Then she returned to the United States. I did kiss her good-bye. She still reminds me that I kissed her as I would have kissed my mother. I was not to return to the United States for two more years. We kept contact by writing.

I then entered a period of profound struggle. Fortunately, I was able to talk openly with many people while traveling and especially with priests at the Casa where I lived in Rome. It was an intense period of self-examination, intellectual growth, and development of self-aware-ness. It was probably the most intense and alive period of my life.

I had not sorted out priesthood, clergy, service to people, and my own needs. These distinctions would be most important in the next few months. They had all been lumped together in my vision as "the way a priest lives." This image started when I met Father Ed Conlin in front of Incarnation rectory at age five and decided to become an altar boy. Family legend says that I wanted to be a priest from the time my mother died when I was three.

Incarnation was a typical large-city parish composed mainly of Irish immigrant families. When I entered the seminary I was the pride of the family. I worked in the rectory, planned altar-boy meetings, and helped priests in all sorts of ways. Father Ivan Illich, an assistant in the parish, introduced me to work among the newly arriving Puerto Rican com-munity.

Thus, I was in familiar contact with priests. I knew how busy they were and how many demands were made on them. I knew how tired they could be and how much they could accomplish. I was not aware that I was not exposed to the inner struggles with which they lived. Nor did I realize that Incarnation parish was not typical and not in touch with the mainstream of our society. Rome gave me an opportunity to fill in gaps in my intellectual life and to meet someone like Dianne. Europe helped put me in touch with the mainstream of society. Several experiences illustrate what was awakened within me.

During my first months in Rome I searched for a parish where I might spend Christmas in order to practice Italian. A priest from New

York suggested I contact Luigi Rosadoni, pastor of a small parish on the outskirts of Florence. I did so and he quickly replied that he would be most happy to have me.

I anticipated two weeks in a fairly traditional parish. I feared that I wouldn't have much chance to use Italian because priests in Italy have a reputation for being distant from their people. Instead I had a fantastic experience. There was an intense community life. I spent every day from early morning until late at night talking about the Church, American politics and way of life, and the war in Vietnam. I wrote a long letter describing it to relatives and friends when I returned to Rome.

Those weeks were good not only for my Italian but also for the close friendship I formed with Luigi. We talked for many hours. I was most impressed by a sign on his door: "Like everyone else I work from nine to five. I edit books. I pray at eight every evening and celebrate the Eucharist at 7:30 every morning. Come join me if you want to pray. I eat about six each evening. Bring your food and join me if you want to talk."

Sharing with Luigi, I had my first experience with a man engaged in the process of changing the structure within which he had to work. I saw the enormous opposition his efforts generated. I shared with him his uncertainty and yet his courageous determination. I felt for the first time I had really come in contact with a group that was doing the work of Christ. I could identify Luigi with Christ as a champion of the freedom of men and the rights of the poor in opposition to the existing establishment.

A few months later I went with a group of American teachers to the Soviet Union and other communist countries. Again, it was a moving event in my life. A day spent at a Moscow public school made me realize the unity that existed among us as individuals in spite of political ideologies. The experience awakened me to the reality that institutions designed to help people can create divisions when they become more interested in the institution than in the people.

After my summer of travel, my letter to friends in the United States said in part: "I am convinced that it is all but impossible for the Church to be highly centralized and guided by a uniform set of laws and still follow Christ. The freedom that marked Christ's life, that made him the perfection of human fulfillment cannot exist in such a highly centralized system." The same letter shows what I was thinking about clergy: "For three months I was away completely from a clerical environment. I lived completely in the secular world and I found (as it said way back in Genesis) that it was good. I became more aware than ever that even with the best of intentions, the clergy often live in a world apart with an almost completely closed circuit of ideas and concepts. The priest must be completely immersed in the Christian community and the world in which it lives if the community is truly to grow from within and not be imposed from without."

That letter was written in October immediately after my return to Rome. I was ready for a year of study. Then it started. In rapid-fire succession I discovered that two of my closest friends had resigned the priesthood and that a third was on the verge of resigning. The last was a man whom a New York bishop had described to me as one of the few really honest men in the diocese.

I wrote to Ivan Illich, director of the Center for Intercultural Formation at Cuernavaca, Mexico, asking his ideas about married clergy and the way to bring it about. His reply jolted me: The problem was not the existence of celibate priests but of a clerical mentality. The reply incorporated the ideas he later published in *Critic* under the title "The Vanishing Clergyman." In essence I understood him to say that while there would eventually be a married priesthood, he hoped that none of the present clergy would ever be allowed to enter that group because changing in that way would preserve the clerical mentality.

I rebelled against the implicit suggestion that I, trapped by the system, could never function as a priest apart from a clerical mentality. The more I thought about it, however, the more I realized that my objections were against the structures that kept priests apart from people, that what I really wanted was the end of a *clerical* priesthood. This realization enabled me to think of a priesthood not bound by clerical traditions and structures but free to develop whatever style of life was helpful.

At the time that this distinction became clear to me, I had the experience with a number of priests at the Casa of trying to express to our bishops our concern over the Church's position regarding birth control. We were not attempting to resolve the issue. In the fall of 1966 we were concerned that Vatican statements, saying both that the Church was in no doubt and that a decision would be made as soon as possible, made the Church look foolish. We decided to send a confidential expression of our opinion to the executive board of the American hierarchy.

The fear I discovered within myself and so many others, while in the process of formulating and sending a simple expression of our understanding, made me more frightened than ever at the situation I found myself in as a priest. I began to feel that I was constantly under pressure to sell my integrity in favor of preserving my place in a system.

Early in December I received word that my third friend had resigned from the priesthood. In addition I read an article in *Jubilee* suggesting a way in which the Church could move toward a married clergy as a form of Priesthood for the Future.

I had been tempted to return to the United States to see Dianne, but we had ruled that out as too difficult emotionally and too expensive. With this latest news I decided that I had to return for Christmas vacation. I wrote the New York chancery indicating that I was returning to see my friends who had resigned, to discuss the possibility of finishing my thesis at Catholic University in Washington, and finally to discover what was happening in the American Church. It was impossible to write a thesis on the American parish at such a distance.

I arrived in New York in mid-December. I discovered that the cardinal was very upset because of the letter to the bishops and because I had returned without requesting permission. I was told that I could not return to Rome. In January I was assigned to St. Barnabas parish in the Bronx.

Discussions with priests in the diocese revealed the same unrest that I had experienced. My struggle was not the result of special experiences but were common among priests.

My return enabled me to resume contact with Dianne. She was studying in upstate New York, and so we saw each other only once a month until the following fall when she moved to the city. Marriage was still on my mind. But I knew that I could not decide about marriage until I had made some definite decisions about my role as a priest and my place in the diocese.

At this time I also became aware of a group known as the National Association for Pastoral Renewal, which had been formed to create a public discussion of celibacy. Apparently a number of people reading the same *Jubilee* article I had seen wanted to do something to make it a reality. Through a classmate I got in touch with Bob Francoeur and Carl Hemmer, who were doing much of the organizing work. I began to help in every way I could, both in New York and on the national level. This made my position in the diocese more difficult than ever.

Meanwhile, I was also working at St. Barnabas, which was very similar to my home parish, Incarnation. I found people with real needs. Many could never change their understanding of the Church. There was an important role for someone to provide the services they needed. However, I decided I could not do that work. It seemed much more important to me to work toward forming an association that would voice the discontent of so many priests in New York and to continue my work with NAPR on the discussion of celibacy.

I did all that was expected of me at Barnabas, and I have no hesitation in saying that I did it well. My sermons were well prepared and stimulating. I used spare time for my other activities. I felt more and more that the forces keeping Barnabas from being a real community could not be solved at Barnabas. Larger aspects of Church structure had to change first.

That September I attended the Symposium on Clerical Celibacy at Notre Dame University and was elected treasurer of NAPR. When I left for the symposium, I knew that I would have to resign at some point in the near future. My effectiveness within the structure of the New York archdiocese was diminished by the fact that I had opened discussion on so many touchy topics. Moreover, I was becoming increasingly aware that only by being myself did I really influence people. Openly expressing my own needs for greater freedom in my style of life and my own desire for marriage helped others to be more aware of their own feelings and more open in talking about them.

One priest told me that before I left for Rome, he had been fearful of sharing his feelings with me because I seemed so much a part of the system: a top man in the seminary, close to people in the chancery, and chosen for special studies. Experiences such as this made me feel more and more that the greatest contribution I could make would be to express openly what I felt myself to be.

Returning from Notre Dame, I discovered a letter transferring me back to St. Ann's on East Twelfth. I was furious. I had asked for a parish such as Barnabas because I felt that the problems of areas like St. Ann's were not internal but the result of racist attitudes in all-white areas such as Barnabas.

It was a transfer without consultation! I was ready to resign at that moment. But patience won out. If I was going to resign, I wanted every-one to know why; I did not want my action to be written off as an act done in anger. I spoke with Bishop Maguire, the coadjutor archbishop. He told me my ability in Spanish was needed on the Lower East Side. There was nothing that could be done about the transfer, and I made the move to St. Ann's. Rumors were rampant that I had resigned. I visited Puerto Rico to regain my fluency in Spanish and tried to get into the spirit of the work. Still I was frustrated. It now became clear that I would be able to accomplish very little within the system.

On November 1, 1967, I announced my decision to Archbishop Maguire in the form of a letter of resignation and request for laicization. I sent copies of the letter to 150 friends and relatives. I quoted part of it in opening this article, but two other sections seem equally important: "I do not view my decision as a refusal to participate in the process of change. I see it rather as an integral part of the whole process. I feel very deeply that the Spirit acts in many different ways, and in leading each person to the deepest expression of himself, he moves the whole community to greater richness."

Regarding my future I said: "I plan to remain in New York. I feel sure that the age is past when a decision such as this means that one must sever all connections with the past. I value the friendships that have been formed over the course of many years. Most importantly, I remain fully committed to Christ. I am deeply aware that I must con-tinue the effort to discern the will of the Spirit and follow Him wherever He may lead in making the love of Christ more manifest among men."

The response to my decision was most unexpected. More than 130 responded by letter, and many of the others I saw in person. Only two or three were mildly critical. Almost all included an invitation to dinner. I was stunned.

A few weeks later I was offered the position of full-time coordinator of the National Association for Pastoral Renewal. Suddenly, I was in a position to do the things I had wanted to do and had been trying to do in the parish: to work for renewal in the Church.

Progress on my request for laicization has been paralyzed by my refusal to cooperate with many aspects of the present procedure which I consider degrading. A large part of my present work with NAPR is directed toward creating a procedure which will treat men with dignity and respect.

It is difficult to express the factors that lead one to an important personal decision. However, there arrive moments at which struggle ends and a path becomes clear. Such a moment came for me in November 1967. Dianne and I were married the following June. The eight intervening months were filled with self-discovery and the freedom so important for a decision about marriage. I feel that our life together, my studies in Human Relations at New York University, and my work with NAPR will all help me to continue my life with the same Spirit that led me to ordination.

6

A CONTINUING
VOCATION

by James F. Drane

James F. Drane was born on April 6, 1930, in Chester,
Pennsylvania. He was educated at Little Rock College,
Arkansas, where he received his B.A. in philosophy in
1951. He then studied at the Gregorian University in
Rome, receiving his B.D. degree in theology. Especially
interested in languages, he attended Middlebury College
in Vermont, where he received the M.A. in romance languages.

From 1962 to 1964 he studied at the University of
Madrid, where he received his Ph.D., writing his doctoral
dissertation on *Tolerance and Religious Liberty*. Dr.
Drane at present is doing postdoctoral research in philosophy at Yale, where he holds a fellowship. Dr. Drane
taught at St. John's Seminary, Little Rock, and has also
taught at Yale. He is the author of *Pilgrimage to Utopia*
and *Authority and Institution*, and has written numerous
articles for scholarly journals.

He is fluent in Spanish, Italian, French, and Latin, and
has a working knowledge of Portuguese, Romanian, and

Greek, and has done extensive traveling throughout Europe, the Soviet Union, Africa, Asia, and South America.

He served as special language assistant to Cardinal Spellman on his 1958 European tour. He was a special consultant to the Spanish hierarchy on religious liberty in 1963 and was a visiting scholar at Union Theological Seminary in 1966. He was elected that year as president of the Alumni Association of St. John's Seminary, Little Rock.

His book *Authority and Institution* is a study of the concept of authority and its relationship to the varying kinds of institutional forms. It analyzes the organizational patterns of the Catholic Church and the authority characteristics which accompany these patterns. Alternate structural possibilities as well as different styles of leadership are suggested to replace present disfunctional forms.

Since writing his story, Dr. Drane has received dispensation from celibacy.

I never wanted to be anything but a priest. This aspiration goes back to my earliest childhood memories and stayed with me through every period of my life. Even before I can remember, my mother tells me that I used to walk up and down the upstairs hall "reading" my breviary in imitation of the priest.

I managed to work myself into the altar-boy ranks a year ahead of the other kids, learning my Latin responses with the help of a priest uncle whom I dearly loved. Whenever there was a funeral or a wedding, Sister would call me out to serve—a privilege I cherished then, but looking back I think I could have profited by a little more school.

High-school days brought the usual distaff distractions and an explosion of social life. The other candidates for the priesthood from my senior class won scholastic honors. My only distinction was being named "high-school girls' favorite." The idea of the seminary scared me to death, but I gritted my teeth—said good-bye to the dances, turned my zoot suits over to some friends, and headed for St. John's in Little Rock, Arkansas.

My arrival at this old-style "closed" seminary was a culture shock, but I got over it quickly and even came to like my black suit and square-buttoned trousers. After four happy years at St. John's I was sent to Rome for theology, and although the spaghetti never did agree with my Irish stomach (which had been primed on potatoes and gravy), I loved Rome and the Italians. I preached in Italian at one of my first masses and all the old ladies thought I was one of their own.

My one and only assignment as a priest was to the faculty of St. John's Seminary, where I spent twelve very happy years. It was there in June 1967 that I got a letter from the bishop which read, "This is to inform you that you are relieved of any position in connection with St. John's Seminary and of any further service to the Church in the Diocese. It would evidently be inconsistent to use the services of a priest to represent the Church when you do not believe what the Church teaches." Farther down the page the bishop continued, "I will be unable to recommend you to any bishop for priestly work in his diocese."

In a letter which followed the next day, the bishop further specified that I was suspect of heresy and warned of the consequences of Canon 2315. Finally I was admonished of the possibility of still another censure "if you should write or speak publically concerning any religious teaching of the Catholic Church."

I have no story to tell of the dissolution of a priestly vocation or commitment to the Church. I was as happy as a priest (and I hope as committed) the day I received my walking papers as when I was first ordained. My separation from the active ministry was unexpected and accompanied by bitter tears. Today I am laicized but I still want to be a priest. I hope I'm not kidding myself when I think that surely someday I'll be back.

Looking back now from the vantage point provided by a couple of years, the whole affair looks silly—perhaps insane. I had disagreed with the bishop on many issues—race, war, ecumenism, philosophy—but the disagreements were never such as to dissolve our friendship. He is, however, admittedly a very conservative man, and the publication of a series of articles entitled "Natural Law, Papal Authority, and Birth Control" in the Arkansas *Gazette* touched on what he considered to be defined essentials of the faith. He felt that he had no alternative but to eliminate me.

It all looks absurd because since then the leading moral theologians in the Church have said what I did and more. Hundreds of priest theologians in this country have stated much stronger views than mine. Half the priests in the United States hold the same opinion as myself on this question. About 80 percent of the laymen in the Church in child-bearing years practice what I advocated.

National hierarchies in the major western European countries have insisted that this issue does not belong to the essence of our faith and have asked those who disagree with the official Church position and act according to their conscience not to absent themselves from the sacraments or feel in any way alienated from the Church. With me it was more a question of where I spoke and when I declared myself on the problem of birth control.

It would be of little interest to go into exactly what I wrote. Generally the articles outlined the meaning of natural-law theory and showed that the principles of natural law in no way dictate one and only one answer on birth control. The Church was not stuck with the proscriptions against contraception, I argued, because a more adequate natural-law theory pointed to liberal alternatives to the old rules.

The bishop took strongest exception to what I said about the papacy, and this I feel may turn out to be the truest thing I wrote. The papacy, I insisted, was being victimized and distorted by a myth—that of a sacral figure, with a pipeline to God, issuing infallible declaration on any and every issue. This is not the Christian papacy. It is an unscriptural, theologically unfounded myth which unfortunately persists in the minds of Protestants and Catholics alike.

This pagan image of the Pope can be laid to rest, I said, only by some solemn pronouncement of a Pope which everyone recognizes as fallible. Paul VI, I predicted, could very well be the Pope who would return the papacy to a more modest, more Christian, more scriptural understanding of itself by a solemnly pronounced mistake on birth control.

The Pope has made that statement, and I am optimistic that out of it will emerge a papacy no longer burdened by the old myth, more acceptable to Christians outside the Catholic family, and ultimately a much more effective instrument of good. All this, however, is part of another long story.

Everything that happened to me after publishing the articles is understandable once we recognize that the Church is different from place to place. We do not live in all places at all times as individuals, and neither does the institutional Church. Someday this whole birth-control question will be settled and forgotten.

Soon, very soon, dissent from what is now the official position will be guaranteed for all the faithful and no longer any reason for recriminations or punishment. In the meantime, however, we have to live where we are and with the circumstances which surround our particular condition. The big choice is not when or where we live out our lives as Christians, but how we react to what situations we meet.

In telling my story, I must avoid creating the impression that I'm the good guy and the hierarchs all wear black hats. That would be untrue. Equally untrue would be the impression that in my particular situation I really had no choice but to do what I did.

I have my pangs of conscience and feelings of guilt for the affair (just being in conflict with the official Church makes me feel guilty). I also have reservations about my personal decisions. Someday I could be very, very sorry for the path I have chosen, but I pray that God will salvage even my sins and errors. Ultimately I am sure it will all turn out well because for a Christian there can be no final tragedy.

When all the hoopla over my firing quieted in the press and the protests from the laity began gathering dust on the bishop's desk, I turned to a legal appeal. Father Walter Clancy, a colleague at the seminary (who had been a close friend for more years than either of us like to count), and I decided to work up a formal case against my punishment to submit to Rome.

We didn't bother with the issue of birth control, but rather concentrated on the Canon laws which were violated in the procedure of my being fired without warning and without even a token attempt to sit down to talk over the grievance. The case was an impressive one, running some sixty-five pages of close legal reasoning with multiple citations from commentaries. I wrote a cover letter in Italian to the head of the Congregation of the Holy Office pleading for a sympathetic hearing and sent everything off air mail special delivery to Rome. Then began the long wait for a reply.

My trouble with the Church began in mid-summer, and by the time I had exhausted all available channels of appeal, September was approaching. I found out much later that legally I had a right to room, board, and salary until the formal appeal was decided, but at the time

I felt under pressure to get out. The bishop had closed the whole seminary soon after my firing, and the rooms I occupied were assigned to one of the chancery officials.

Providentially I got a postdoctoral research fellowship from the philosophy department at Yale University, which at least gave me a place to be. Jim Gustafson, the professor of Christian Ethics and head of the religious studies department, had been a big help to me all during the summer crisis, and he was instrumental in arranging the invitation. I guess I'll never forget the day I packed my things and left the seminary where I had spent twenty years of my life. Yale was a good place to be going to, but it would be a while before I would feel wholly myself there. Part of me was left behind forever.

One of the advantages of celibate life as it is structured for the priest by the Church is a freedom from economic need. I never had a cent and yet always seemed to have more than enough for everything. I never bothered with social security or retirement plans or savings of any sort. That small bit of unworldly trust was the least I felt I could do after having promised to take Christ as my inheritance. My firing and separation from the priesthood, then, caught me with a bad case of financial embarrassment. My Catholic friends were all praying hard for me, and my Jewish friends, as soon as they heard I had a chance to go to school, started collecting funds. The rabbi was the treasurer of the drive, and money was sent to me through a Protestant charitable society.

At Yale I studied very hard, kept very close to the sacraments, and made some lasting new friendships. The unresolved situation with the Church, however, lay on me like a heavy weight. I didn't want to live out my life in the limbo to which I had been assigned as a suspended priest. I had no idea where I was going or what was in store for me. I never knew what to call myself or how to explain my status. The Church was important to me and I wanted a place and a role. Being suspended, silenced, and cut off from priestly functions was like being in jail. Life for me must have a project, and I felt as though mine had gone and that I was treading water. Worst of all was the fact that I had no idea how long this situation would last. As the months went by without a word from the Church, I began to entertain the idea of becoming a layman.

The idea of not being a priest was like thinking the unthinkable for me. The priesthood was part of my personal identity, and I had trouble even imagining myself as anything else. Silly as it may sound, putting on a suit and tie created for me a real trauma. A few weeks after my arrival at Yale I had to give a public lecture which required that I dress up. When I looked at myself in secular clothes, I got sick to my stomach. I literally did not recognize myself. Had it not been for the fact that people were waiting, I would never have gone out that night.

As time passed, however, I began to get accustomed to nonclerical clothes and even to the layman's role at Mass. One of the most interesting adjustments was listening to sermons. I would sit through most, either figuring out what I would have said or thinking: "Why begin with such a dull opener?" "Oh, no, don't give them that old stuff." "Stop there—that's enough. It's too long already." "You're getting off the point again."

During the year I sought counsel and advice on my situation from good friends and trusted spiritual directors. Once I flew out West to spend a few days in a monastery, praying and talking over my dilemma. There comes a time, however, when a decision must be made, and then it is just you—all alone—before God, who has to make a step in one or another direction. I wrote, finally, asking to be laicized.

There were other options open to me, but none looked reasonable. My health had begun to deteriorate under all the strain of the waiting, the uncertainties, the separation from my life's work. The doctor was giving me pills for my stomach, sleeping pills, tranquilizers, and they were having less and less effect.

I could have continued to wait, but that was painful, especially since there was that very real fear that my case would simply never come up. Not even having received notice of the case being received did not inspire confidence in the juridical processes. Those who thought I might ultimately hear from the appeal held out no hope that it could be decided in my favor. No matter how strong the arguments, they said, the bishop was bound to be upheld. Even if I managed somehow to win, I knew that there would be conditions placed on my being reinstated, ones which I very likely could not in conscience accept. Were I to lose the case, I would have to retract in order to get back, and that I could not do.

The most serious alternative to my decision to ask out was the option of waiting. If I waited long enough, surely something would happen. The bishop had refused even to permit me to go to another diocese. But he would surely reconsider that harsh measure after a while, especially if I could find some bishop who needed a priest badly enough to take me. There would, however, always be that one condition hanging over my head—that is, "Do not write, do not talk about anything controversial." I could just see a bishop telling me, "Now that we have taken you back and given you another chance, behave yourself. Stay away from anything controversial, just do your job."

The trouble was that I could never reconcile "my job" with just being a ritual priest. A vocation to the priesthood couldn't mean submerging oneself into all the institutional patterns of Church as we know it. If the priestly vocation is a call to conform to things as they are, then God is calling men to immaturity and to a diminished humaneness. A vocation to serve the Church had to be a call to imitate our Lord, and Christ was no conformist, nor was He a great respecter of tradition, nor was He particularly impressed with either the religious or secular authorities of His day. It would be dangerous for any priest to confuse himself with his master, but there are times in his life when he might feel something needs to be said, something official needs to be changed. Certainly he must be reasonable. He must seek out the reasons behind the institutions, the laws to which he objects, and be respectful of the wisdom and opinions of others. But a vocation to the priesthood must not preclude the possibility of a priest standing on his own feet and following his conscience when the issue is pressing and the good of the Christian community is at stake.

More months passed with no word on the laicization. Following his conscience, the bishop could neither permit me to function as a priest or permit me to be laicized, so he sent my petition to the apostolic delegate. Very soon after Archbishop Raimondi entered the picture as the new apostolic delegate, I got an unexpected answer from the earlier legal appeal to Rome against my suspension. The decision was sent not to me but to the bishop, who forwarded a copy of the decree. It was short and so I quote the whole letter (translation mine).

"Most Excellent and Most Reverend Lord [it was addressed to the Bishop]: This sacred congregation diligently considered the case of the priest James Drane, in which your Most Reverend Excellency tried to combat errors affirmed and publicly diffused by him.

"The examination having been completed, the most excellent father of this sacred consistory on the 3rd of April agreed that the priest

Drane was justly punished by Your Excellency. It is moreover the mind of the sacred congregation that Your Excellency, with your praiseworthy portrayal of solicitude, use every means to keep the priest Drane from seeking reduction to the lay state but that despite everything he be recalled to his priestly ministry and function in the future as a good priest."

The bishop did exactly as instructed and did so with all goodwill. In his own letter accompanying the Roman decree he asked me to accept the decision and return to the priesthood where I had been so happy. The conditions were: public profession of belief in the supreme teaching authority of the Holy Father and retraction of my views on birth control. "If you can do these two things, I would certainly be most happy and most willing to have you back as a member of our diocesan family," he said. "Come back Fr. Jimmy," he concluded, "while there is still time."

The bishop's letter really pointed up the tragedy of our difficulties. We both wanted to live the faith and be loyal to the Church. For him, however, faith was acceptance of every teaching and tradition with the same religious assent. Faith and loyalty to the Church for him meant willingness to conform to official positions, no matter how strongly one felt.

To me this was immoral. It was in my opinion an altogether misguided notion of loyalty to hold up blind obedience as a Catholic ideal. If the Church has a human side and its share of sin, then loyalty may in some circumstances require saying no, even to what has been canonized as the "official position."

The bishop and I both are believers, but our experience of Christian life is different. Our notion of what it means to be a man of faith is different and therefore we have an irreconcilable conflict over how to best live out a commitment to Christ within the Church. Our problem is the problem of the Church today. As long as one or another side in the controversy insists on being entirely right, very understandable differences of opinion lead to scandalous abuses of authority—punishments, alienations, and suffering. Certainly the community of love could get along with different experiences of how to be a Christian. After all, St. Peter and St. Paul had some fundamental disagreements on what the Christian life was all about and managed to work together in Christian charity.

After the Roman decision, I made another appeal to be laicized. The Pope had come out with his encyclical on birth control and all hopes of coming to some understanding was gone. The bishop followed the encyclical with a pastoral letter in which he made obedience a condition for being a Catholic. Those who had "misled" the faithful into thinking that a change on this issue was possible were branded as enemies of the Church and subverters of the word of God. The day that letter was read at every Mass happened to be my first Sunday back in the diocese since the suspension. The letter was followed up with a sermon at the Mass I attended, in which I was roundly condemned as an enemy of the Church. It was sure nice to be home.

After another wait and many exchanges of letters, I received a short note from Archbishop Raimondi. In it he informed me that the Holy Father had approved the decree "reducing me to the lay state," but that I had not been dispensed from celibacy. Furthermore, I was advised that "this measure was in no way to be construed as a penal matter, but rather as a sign of clemency and mercy of the Church which wishes to offer relief to one of Her sons at a time of crisis."

After all that had happened it was impossible for me to see any clemency or mercy in that decree. I never wanted to be separated from the priesthood, and now I was facing the possibility of separation from the Church. The condition for my being a Catholic layman was that I live out my life in a queer intermediate state—not a priest but living as one—a layman but without the right to live as a layman. My membership in the Church was made conditional upon my giving up what is universally agreed is a natural right of every layman. I refused to accept that condition. Having exhausted all the normal channels I wrote a letter to the Pope personally and asked him to relieve me of this unnatural burden.

A writing assignment brought me to Rome unexpectedly and I dropped in at the Congregation for the Doctrine of the Faith (Holy Office) and the surprise of my life. The priests with whom I spoke were very understanding and very considerate. They assured me that full laicization could be expected in a month. We talked for hours about the problems in today's Church and they showed anxiousness to find ways of humanizing the old ways of handling priest problems.

As I sat in a dark and dreary room of that dismal building with its ominous reputation and exchanged thoughts on the Church freely with a warm and friendly official of the Curia, I thought to myself that passé structures like old trees sometimes produce late fruits which are beautiful. Just when one is tempted to think there is no hope, hope springs up from an unexpected source. I have no hope for the Holy Office, but that young Curia monsignor gave me all kinds of hope that the Church will survive the present travail.

Once that crisis was over a whole new set of problems emerged. What now will I do with my life? I became a priest because I wanted to give my life away—to do the generous thing. To have returned to the priestly forms against my conscience would in a sense have been to fall away from that vocational aspiration. I feel weak and unprepared for a generous life because without knowing it, I had grown selfish as a priest. Everything was provided for me, and I had become accustomed to the smooth way which had always been opened up to me. Starting out anew without the supports of the clerical state makes me feel like Linus, forced to step out into the cold cruel world without the blanket. I am full of insecurity.

As a priest, I had a professional security which is now gone. I knew what being a priest was like. I could do what being a priest required, and people recognized me as a competent member of an established profession. The professional status opened many doors which are now closed to me as a layman. A phone call which opened with the words "This is Father Drane" assured attention and courtesy. A great deal of good can be done by a priest just because he belongs to a trusted profession. All those possibilities are gone along with all the deference given to the priestly office.

Gone, too, is the economic security. Although I never had any money to speak of, I never felt economically insecure. All the essentials and more than my share of the incidentals were provided for me. Not even the greatest enemy of the Church ever entertained any notion of her going out of business or laying anyone off. Now all that I had grown to take for granted I have to provide for myself: room, board, telephone, paper, cleaning, laundry, stationary. I knew a great change had taken place a week after arriving at Yale, when I had to go to the Laundromat to do my own washing and pay for it to boot.

Getting a job is a problem, too. I always thought I worked hard as a priest, but was it hard enough? When I got tired or felt a little sick, I could always take a day off. But what was considered an exceptional effort then is now considered to be normal. Working conditions will never be like the seminary either, where I lived with priests who were kind and considerate and where I had a very good boss. (I'll miss especially those late evening get-togethers for drinks and laughs with priest friends.) The game of stepping on the next guy to get ahead and getting stepped on in the process is not one for which I feel at all prepared.

Then, too, there is the social problem. I do not want to go away from Little Rock where I lived all my adult life. I don't want to live in exile. The Church must grow up to accept conflict, differences of opinion, even changes of vocation, and I would like to try making a contribution toward this broader mentality by staying in my own community.

I have many uncertainties, but in my stronger moments I feel sure that even my fellow Catholics will get over the shock of a laicized priest. I know there will be embarrassment for a time. We'll all feel a little strained and uncomfortable, but that will pass. Surely, I could do some good as a layman in the community which once I served as a priest.

Finally there is the worry and the fears about marriage. Most priests leaving these days are doing so because they find life as a celibate having a crippling and destructive effect on their lives. They rightly call attention to the fact that the isolated seminary life to which there was added the subtle yet constant conditioning against married life does not prepare a person for making a mature decision in favor of the celibate life. Many times, however, the choice of celibacy, like the choice to marry, though not mature, turns out to be one a person can live with and in which he can fulfill himself.

There has to be constant adjustment in the motivation for celibacy because the initial reasons for embracing it show up as childish and insufficient not long after ordination. Exactly the same thing, however, is true of most marriages. There remain, nevertheless, continually valid reasons for a celibate life, which justify it for some and make it a fruitful and fulfilling life.

I made the commitment because I wanted to be a priest, and celibacy was part of the package. This is the most common and the weakest reason. Added to this is usually the ideal of giving everything away—making the total gift of one's life. Paradoxically, however, as a priest grows older in the celibate life he sometimes sees himself becoming more selfish. He is thrown up against case after case of the married man who did not enter marriage with the motive of a total self-forgetting. But as the children come along and the demands upon him increase, he winds up living out in practice the selfless generosity and dedication to others, which constituted the priest's ideal.

The priest, who gave up everything to be free for others, ends up giving in more and more to the uninterrupting onslaughts of his selfish nature. Given the choice between a good and a bad bottle of wine, he tends, like others of his species, to take the good one. His meals tend to be the best that money can buy. The same is true of his clothes and his car. Since he manages his own time for the most part, he gives himself more and more time off. His vacations would be the envy of many married men, and there are many hours in his day given over to the paper, magazines, siesta, and T.V. Some priests use the extra time afforded them by the lack of parental responsibility for extra work, but there are others who do not swim as well against the tide.

Nonetheless one can continue to put up defenses against the selfish orientations of the celibate life, and the ideal of total giving can continue to inspire and fulfill the priest. The celibate life need not be one of frustration, and it can be lived out without compromise or disintegration. My departure from the active priesthood, then, is not the protest against celibacy, although I sympathize with the priests who leave for that reason. An optional celibacy is the only reasonable institution for the clergy and must be the rule before too long.

Once removed from the active ministry, however, celibacy makes no sense without a special vocation. Giving myself in love to another seems the only normal way to love God and lead a decent human life. Marriage appears now as a step toward maturity and unselfishness. To remain celibate would be to place myself in the near occasion of a selfish and un-Christlike life. Seeing the reality, however, is one thing, taking the step quite another. My good mother and my nine brothers and sisters suffered through this trial with me. Their continuing encouragement gives me the freedom and the courage at least to consider this step which never before was a live option for me as a priest.

One last word about the priesthood and the Church today. It is not just the priest who is in crisis today, but medical doctor, psychiatrist, policeman, university professor, and many others. These are changing times and many professors are caught in the change. The problem is not a dissolution of authority or a new wave of individualism but rather something much more basic. Priests are separated from bishops most frequently because they have different experiences with the Christian life.

The bishop experiences the Gospel and the Christian message one way, the younger priest in a totally different way. The bishop seeks to promote those structures and institutions which correspond to his vision of the faith. Priests attack those same structures and institutions because they cripple and impede the way they see and live the Gospel. We need something like a new Pentacost to bring our understandings of the Christian reality closer together and a big dose of political imagination to adjust our institutional forms to this reality.

This is the story of change in one human life. The change has been a radical one, and yet there are some continuities. It is the same person trying to continue to live out an unchanging commitment made years ago, despite the strange shifts in the style of life this seems to require. Living out a commitment means choice—constant choice. The world in which we live is a fallen world, and this fallen estate is never more evident than in cases of important human decisions.

Because the world is fallen, the choices which confront man are never black and white. If I had chosen to wait it out as a suspended priest, I could have done some good. Even a lifetime seemingly wasted can be a witness to important values, and by choosing to be laicized, this good will go unrealized. At the same time the choice to become a layman offers possibilities for another type of witness, to different values, which may be even more important for the needs of today's Church. In conflict situations we see clearly that, try as we may to avoid it, we inevitably do some harm and fail to do some good by every choice. There is just no way to choose so as to do only the good. Even when we think we have a clean-cut choice for good, our internal motives are not always lily white.

Realizing that our choices are linked to a combination of good and bad effects and that our motives are not always completely pure cannot, however, keep us from choosing. We can't cop out. Tangled in a web of internal and external unrighteousness, we have to make our life decisions. I cannot stand before God, as Luther did, and say: "Here I stand. I can do no other."

I could have done other. What I chose, however, was not only in good conscience but with an eye to what I thought was best for the Church. I may have been mistaken, but God does not insist upon our always being right. Even our conscious faults can be the occasion for His gracious forgiveness. I admit to my share of fears and feelings of inadequacy, but I do not feel uncertain about my relationship with God. Confident of His mercy and His love, I have no fear of God's judgment.

7

A PRIESTHOOD
FOR TOMORROW

by Eugene C. Bianchi

Born in Oakland, California, on May 5, 1930, Eugene Carl
Bianchi studied at Gonzaga University, Spokane, where
he received the B.A. and M.A. degrees. He later studied
at the College St-Albert, Louvain, Belgium, where he was
awarded the Licentiate in Sacred Theology, *cum laude.*
In 1966 he received his Ph.D. from Columbia University–
Union Theological Seminary, New York.

  He served as visiting professor in the summer of 1966
at the graduate school of theology at the University of San
Francisco. During the two following years he was assistant
professor of religious studies at the University of Santa
Clara, where he was also the director of the Center for
the Study of Contemporary Values. From 1963 to 1966
Dr. Bianchi was assistant editor of *America,* a national
Catholic weekly edited by the Jesuits in New York. He
is at present assistant professor of religion at Emory University, Atlanta, Georgia.

  Dr. Bianchi has published numerous articles in various
learned journals and is the author of *John XXIII and*

American Protestants and *The Worldly Church* and the
editor of the volume *Christian-Marxist Dialogue*. He has
contributed a chapter on the impact of modern pluralism
on Roman Catholic teaching, published in a collection on
pluralism and religion from the Jewish Theological Seminary of America. He has also contributed a chapter to
The Ecumenical Plateau, a symposium on the challenge
to the Church today, published in both England and the
United States. Dr. Bianchi has published book reviews
in many learned journals in this country and abroad.

In the summer of 1968 I took a leave of absence from the California
province of the Jesuit Order. I had been ordained to the priesthood
for seven years when I took this step, and had been most recently
teaching theology at the University of Santa Clara. In this essay I
would like to reflect on some personal motivations that led me to move
in this new direction. If I thought that these reflections were simply
unique to myself, it would not be worth belaboring the reader. However, I believe that thoughts like mine are becoming more widespread
among both Catholic clergy and Catholic laity. Therefore, I write in
the hope that these reflections will make a modest contribution to the
present dialogue about freer and more adapted ways of living the
priesthood in the Roman Catholic Church.

My early years were fairly typical as background for an American
priest. Most of the landmarks were there in proper order: Catholic
grammar school, altar boy, Jesuit high school, and entrance into the
novitiate at Los Gatos, California. My prenovitiate years were certainly
not a cloistered time. Sports, extracurricular and social activities, and
a job with a chain men's store helped broaden my outlook. I was moved
by the idealism of a priestly life of service, following in the footsteps
of a few Jesuit high-school teachers who influenced me.

But in many ways it was a closed world. In addition to the ordinary
limitations of a high-school graduate, the early years of Jesuit training
were very isolated and restrictive. I am grateful for the many benefits
that came to me as student and high-school teacher during those first

ten years, but they were all very much under the dominance of the vintage Catholicism we then knew.

Four years in Louvain, Belgium, studying theology expanded my perspectives, largely because this period coincided with the beginnings of Pope John's council. A deeper sense of Gospel freedom contrasted with the structures of Catholicism that we had been taught to view as sacred. My years of doctoral study at Columbia and Union Theological in New York, coupled with the task of helping edit *America,* opened still newer vistas for a freer, more adapted and involved ministry for the Church.

It seems good to state at the beginning an underlying premise of my thinking that has been growing through reading and reflection in recent years. Life is a process, a maturation through new experiences and insights. This implies staying open to new calls, testing them in the Spirit as best one can, but eventually for integrity's sake a man must risk decision. This processive view of life is attacked by some as a cover-up for infidelity. Such persons would cite fidelity to marriage vows as comparable to commitment to priesthood. In this static perspective, the priest who leaves is a defector guilty of instability, infidelity, and dereliction of duty.

Prescinding from the insecurities and closed-mindedness that often accompany such judgments, I would reject the parallel between marriage and priesthood, as though they represented the same situation. The priesthood is a function or ministry which has been and will be exercised in the married as well as in the unmarried state. But even beyond this distinction, a processive attitude toward human development demands a new assessment of the Catholic view on divorce itself. Facile divorce is irresponsible and harmful. But rigid fidelity to an intolerable marriage, which can become a hateful and destructive arrangement, is also an ungodly solution. Catholic theologians and marriage experts are becoming more aware of the need to rethink canon law on questions of marriage and divorce.

A processive view of life neither negates one's past nor does it necessarily imply infidelity to past options. Rather it incorporates the past, as a gift and a responsibility, into a new direction. A processive view of life can also be linked to true fidelity. This means that a person does his best to be faithful to past commitments, both personal and in-

stitutional, but he may eventually have to leave the structural surroundings of the past precisely to be faithful to a new vision.

My own decision to leave the institutional surroundings of the priesthood is ultimately a deeply personal one that I myself will continue to
discover as time passes. My move does not represent a radical and
bitter break with the past. In speech and writing, I have not been more
critical of defects in the Church than other reform-minded priests. My
memories of twenty years as a Jesuit are mostly happy ones. I am grateful for the education provided, the life values and hopes that were
inspired in me, and most of all, for some deep and continuing friendships.

Why, then, the separation? After considerable reflection, I can
discern a cluster of motivations that I have only partially been able to
articulate to myself. There is no iron logic in these views; nor do I see
my way as a formula that others *must* follow, although I feel quite sure
that similar attitudes are now present in many priests and seminarians.

First, I sense a growing need to experiment with freer modes of
living priesthood than those provided in current canonical legislation.
The key word here is freedom. I appreciate the reforms toward greater
adult liberty now in process in both the secular and the religious clergy.
But I think that priestly life in present Catholic institutions is still too
encumbered with laws and life styles that militate against the kind of
personal freedom that is valued by contemporary man. Clerical life in
Catholicism continues to be too bound by monastic and authoritarian
traditions.

Monastic forms of obedience often served older cultures quite well.
Moreover, a serious case can be made for the continuance of the
monastic tradition today, especially if the priesthood were not so
closely identified with it. Characteristic of the monk's heritage is the
high premium placed on docile compliance, which frequently means
obedience to a system of paternalistic authority. These authorities may
be more or less wise and benevolent, but the basic structure is such
that it works against self-determination in important life issues. Such
obedience is propped up with supporting pieties, sanctions, and ex-
hortations to loyalty.

But when examined closely, this obedience is more the product of a
medieval-hierarchical view of Christianity than it is a reflection of the
New Testament. The obedience of Jesus was not primarily to earthly

superiors, but rather to his sense of mission as he progressively became more aware of it. Such obedience is far more open to personal and communal enrichment than the tightly legalized structures that prevail in the Catholic clergy. It would be hard, if not impossible, to justify much of our Canon Law in the light of the Gospel message of freedom in the spirit.

The increased awareness in modern society of the need for greater freedom in opportunities and choices has its effect on the Catholic priest and the layman pondering a priestly ministry. The movement in the clergy toward real participational democracy and toward a wider realm of personal decision-making is part of a much broader cultural drive toward fuller human freedom in contemporary culture. The movement toward freedom and significant representation among priests, as exemplified in the new priests' federations, is very akin to the movements for civil rights among less privileged races and minorities. Through the convergence of many historical factors, an intense new awareness of the need for fuller freedom is spreading in society. I maintain that this growing realization of the need for freer life styles is a way by which God speaks to us through contemporary culture.

The impact of this awareness can be seen in the Catholic clergy's restiveness with older structures and life styles. Unfortunately, most bishops in the United States seem too fearfully wedded to a past world-view to appreciate the depth of the freedom crisis in their clergy. Nor do the bishops seem willing to trust that the cultural freedom movements are part of God's work in current history. Moreover, many priests mistake surface symptoms for the deeper malaise. They expend their energies patching up superficial problems when in fact the whole underlying authority structure is questionable today, because it rests on an outdated historical model. This monarchical and legalistic system is not essential to basic Gospel values, and in many ways hinders witness to such values.

It is also significant that some protest tactics learned from other freedom movements, such as organized demonstrations and common public statements, are being employed by the Catholic clergy. For various reasons priests have been slower to urge their cause toward responsible freedom by using the newer methods. Their past training has made such action appear irreligious and even scandalous. Furthermore, as a class, priests have been more easily intimidated by authori-

ties, because priests lack both financial independence and the affective
support of wife and children needed to challenge the system. The
protests against Paul VI's birth-control letter and the resistance to
ensuing injustices against due process indicate the growing vitality of
the freedom movement among the clergy.

In brief, therefore, my first motive for leaving the present institutional structures of priesthood is the desire to involve myself more
freely and completely in the risks and challenges of being my own
man. A minister of the Gospel today should cultivate solidarity with
his fellow men in the insecurities and promises of freedom. Those who
vow poverty today are often the most removed from solidarity with
the uncertainties of their fellows, because the religious institution ab-
sorbs all the risks. The full risk of free, personal determination in the
human community does not seem possible under older forms of clerical
asylum, except perhaps for a relatively few true charismatics.

A second reason for moving in this new direction concerns the question of celibacy and the need for deeper human affection. I need to
distance myself for a time from traditional priestly roles to be able to
come to a more mature decision as to whether I should marry or remain
celibate. Although I had no immediate intentions of marrying when I
left the Jesuits, I felt that I should place myself in a position from which
I could be both open to and responsible for such an option. It is with
deliberation that I choose the words "responsible for." Many priests
and seminarians today are seeking new levels of rapport with women.
This is, of course, a praiseworthy and rewarding desire. Yet I wonder
how responsible these relations are in terms of the woman involved.
Are these men willing to go all the way in their responsibilities for the
woman, should such a love relationship develop, or are they forced by
institutional bonds to follow less responsible patterns? Men are re-
grettably compelled to compromise between the woman and their
priesthood. Integrity suffers all around. This sad situation will probably
intensify until the time that the Roman Catholic Church opens up the
option of a married priesthood.

At this point it would be well to face a common negative sentiment.
It goes something like this: "You had thirteen years to decide for either
priesthood or marriage. You were old enough and free in your decision."
My answer is twofold. First, if life is a process of new experience and
insights, the option to move in such an important human direction

ought not be closed by ecclesiastical fiat, as is now the case. Secondly, I do not think that most of us were truly free in making the celibate decision. Our whole system of clerical education isolated us psychologically, spiritually, and physically from women.

I would only belabor the obvious if I showed how this isolation was realized at each step of our training. In such a climate a man is at best notionally free, but not experientially free. This educational system was not imposed maliciously, but rather as a holy road to priestly development. I am also aware that Catholic seminary formation has changed importantly in our time. Nevertheless, I seriously question the true freedom of a celibate choice as long as priesthood and marriage remain incompatible modes of life according to church law. Celibacy is not so much chosen, even among many religious, as it is put up with in order to be an ordained minister in the religious order of one's choice.

Many factors have been feeding into my present understanding about the compatibility of priesthood and marriage. In both areas more adequate theologies have been developing, especially since Vatican II. The psychological stresses of modern civilization also compel us to reexamine the human value of the priesthood-celibacy equation. Men today have neither the same outlook on sexuality nor the identical affection needs of men in early medieval Europe, whence our legislation comes. To insist that they do with largely irrelevant arguments in papal encyclicals is to implicitly deny the very historical, developmental genius of the Judeo-Christian tradition. Christian history is not a carrousel on which the horses move to the same music in every age.

It would be worse than naïve to see marriage as a cure-all for the problems of the modern priest. It is worse than naïve, because of the destructive results if woman and children are expected to provide the remedy for psychological problems or plain immaturity. Moreover, the question of meaningful ministries for priests is of even greater importance than the possibility of marriage. Yet groups that presently advocate the establishment of a married priesthood in the Catholic West rightly see the close connection between such a reform and creative new ministries. At first, I thought that the National Association for Pastoral Renewal exaggerated when it continued to focus on optional celibacy for priests. I have since come to believe that stressing the celibacy issue is not an exaggeration.

For a married priesthood would so affect the whole clerical system as we have known it that other reforms would follow of necessity. I feel that high-placed conservatives are well aware of this threat to the system; their staunch, almost frenzied, resistance to change in this area indicates their trepidation. For financial reasons alone, a married clergy would lead to new forms of ministry. A sizable number of married priests would have to earn their livings in professions and occupations not connected with the parochial ministry. This secular experience would engender new ideas for experimental ministries.

Although I am firmly convinced that the values of a married priesthood in our time outweigh the drawbacks, I also respect as a Gospel value a true celibate vocation. We will, however, have a better idea of who the true celibates are after we have opened up again the option of a married priesthood. The only ultimate justification for the celibate option is that it be conducive to love and understanding in the priest. When this human development is found in a priest, his celibacy may, indeed, have great meaning. Yet it seems to me that perhaps the majority of those who choose to be priests are not helped to become more deeply human (to humanize is to Christianize) by the celibate mandate they accept. The celibate gift unto charity cannot be manufactured by the present tightly controlled system of priestly selection and formation.

Why is it so preposterous to suppose that by the mutual sacrifices and sharing of married life, a priest could learn to love more profoundly and sympathize more intensely? Why must we deny the normal way of growing in love and understanding when it comes to the priesthood? I would suggest one reason: a type of supernaturalism, mixed with many strains of world-rejecting and humanity-denying philosophies, that has seeped deeply into the life of Catholic Christianity over the centuries.

This supernatualism negates the basic biblical (especially Hebrew) genius of affirming creation, cosmic and human, as good. Let us learn to listen again to the natural depths and rhythms of our body-persons, and cast aside a stunting supernaturalism that, shored up by oppressive laws, impedes mature growth. It is clearly time for us to recognize that a trusting and inspiring love relationship with a woman has a creative role to play in the ministry of the Catholic priest.

We might further ask ourselves why most bishops are opposed to a married clergy. Surely, part of the answer is a sense of tradition, although tradition is often understood in a static, nonhistorical way. But is there not also a fear of losing control over their priests, of trusting them with too much freedom? In other words, the opposition to a married clergy is a reaffirmation of an authoritarian pattern rooted in a basic mistrust of men. This pattern is predicated on fear, not on Christian hope. It is another example of the siege mentality in which the evil world is always attacking the official (hierarchical) Church. Many hoped that this ghost of Pius IX had been laid by John XXIII and Vatican II, but the ghost dies hard.

The supposedly practical reasons against a married priesthood do not carry much weight. It is said that the priest will not be as free for his ministry. But this freedom for ministry depends to a large extent on the men themselves and their families. If we look around the real Catholic clerical world as it actually is, celibacy rarely qualifies as a good argument for a more efficient use of time. Men who are vitally involved in their ministries will use their time fully, whether they be married or not. One could also argue that those who are especially frustrated because of celibacy will be even less effective in their life commitments. They may wear the official clothing, but their lives are often marked by fruitless diversions and escapes that cloak their excessive loneliness and quiet desperation.

Nor do I believe that it would be very difficult for a great part of the laity to adjust themselves to a married priesthood. I think this is also true of older Catholics. After all, they are our fathers and mothers. Human sexual love for a priest is hardly going to disturb them. The laity is much more disconcerted by meanness or narrow-mindedness in their priests than by the prospect of priests having wives. Those who seem the most perturbed about talk of a married clergy are a goodly number of older ecclesiastics, many of whom are in positions of power.

These officials do not appear to really listen to what younger priests and laymen are thinking and saying on the subject of a married clergy. Nor do they seem willing to explore the experiences of other churches to discover the problems and benefits of a married clergy. Attitudes expressed by Pope Paul in his encyclical on celibacy are insulting to other churches with married ministers. An ecumenical age demands better than this.

I would like to make a final point related to celibacy, but also of much broader significance for the Church. The Church witnesses to

Gospel freedom by what it does, not by pious statements. If it preaches freedom and respect for natural rights to men at large, the Church cannot deny that freedom and those rights in its own household. This is hypocrisy. The right to marry is clearly proclaimed in encyclicals (*Peace on Earth,* John XXIII) and is clearly taken away in other encyclicals (*On Priestly Celibacy,* Paul VI). We cannot speak out of both sides of our mouths and expect men to take us seriously. The Church has had too much pious obscurantism and legalistic edict. We must learn to be more trusting in the Church and give men the broadest possible latitude in making life decisions.

A third motive for my decision is both academic and ecumenical. I have long wanted to teach as a Catholic theologian in a secular or non-Catholic university. Although this work could be done as a Jesuit, I believe that I could accomplish this goal better if I were to operate in a more independent fashion. An important dimension of intellectual freedom is involved in being at once respectful of one's Catholic tradition and yet freed from present clerical restrictions to teach and write with greater liberty.

In other writings I have stated my reasons for abolishing prior censorship in the Church. Here I would simply like to make the very personal observation of how much freer I feel to write what I really believe in this essay than I would have felt in more restrictive clerical surroundings. Environment and life style can emancipate us from the subtle intimidations of big brother or old brother.

Furthermore, I believe that one's life style and involvement in the world have significant effects on the kind of theology one teaches and writes about. Through dialogue with teachers and students at Emory University, my thinking has been challenged and stimulated by contact with very diverse traditions. It seems to me important for the development of the whole Christian tradition that its own scholars be in close dialogue with one another across and beyond denominational lines. But such interaction demands that we move out of our garrisons and encounter not only the scholarly works of the other but also the person of the other in prolonged contact of many life activities. Abstract, distant meetings will result in a very pale ecumenism. Deeper ecumenism calls for a concrete effort to break through the usually accepted textbook differences to encounter the other in those profound motivations that give meaning to his life.

Fourthly, ministry-minded motives have taken on a growing significance in prompting my action. When I say that new styles of living priesthood must be pioneered for the last third of this century, I do not want to derogate from the continuing contribution of present forms of secular and religious priesthood. On the contrary, I believe that the traditional structures will be reformed from within and that many of them will continue to be viable for years to come. But I am also convinced that these forms of priesthood will not be enough for young people in the time ahead. Some of us, especially if we have the credentials to stay in the area of religion, will have to move into a gray zone, somewhat outside the main structures, and experience new ways of living priesthood. Perhaps we will eventually be able to articulate to a newer breed of bishops that it is possible and even desirable for men to live fully in a late-twentieth-century mode and at the same time to be priests.

"Done begins with do," as someone has well phrased it. Not that everyone must do what I do, but some of us will have to. This attitude has been criticized as presenting the Church with a *fait accompli*, before seeking official approval. Yet Church history gives abundant testimony that important reforms do not begin from headquarters. They start rather from the periphery of the Church, sometimes even outside of approved channels, and gradually make their way to the official center for judgment. But authorities cannot judge well from abstract blueprints; they must be able to observe the flesh-and-blood operation. For too long, we American Catholics have failed to learn theologically from our pragmatic heritage of trial and error. It is time that we shelved our European blueprints for priesthood and molded patterns of priesthood that are truly adapted to our own traditions and life styles.

From what I have said above, it should be clear that I do not reject my priesthood. As far as I am concerned, I will always be a priest, even though present legislation may restrict the active and external functioning of my priesthood. I am surprised and gratified by the unforeseen opportunities to exercise my ministry in new ways at Emory and in Atlanta. Just trying to be an honest scholar in this new milieu is itself a primary ministry.

Numerous occasions arise for conversations and consultations with teachers and students. Counseling encounters and even invitations to lecture broaden the scope of my ministry. I like to think of what I am doing as one more form of a worker-priesthood. I foresee the day when priests, holding a variety of secular competences, will be more directly involved in the world and able to minister in far more diverse forms than we have previously known.

For these reasons, I strongly urge priests who leave the traditional ministry not to play the laicization game. Laicization is understandable for those who do not wish to continue as priests. It may also be wise to go through the formalities of laicization to avoid family difficulties and to be in good legal standing with present officialdom. But the growing phenomenon today is that many who leave the traditional forms of ministry want to continue as priests in their new directions.

The only way for this change to be eventually accepted by official Church law is for these priests to band together and make their case heard. If priests can be persuaded to play the laicization game in mind and heart, the clerical box stays closed and officialdom is not effectively urged to change the clerical status quo. Moreover, it perpetuates the wrongheaded notion that these officials are the Church by some divine right and the rest of us pertain to the Church by their sufferance. The sociology of institutions tells us plainly that huge structures like the Catholic Church will not make important changes unless organized efforts are made to educate and persuade. These efforts can take many forms, from learned theological tracts to nondestructive direct action to serious prayer. This venturing in priesthood will call for patience and respect on all sides, and it will carry a definite risk of failure as I move into still uncharted areas.

Some persons will not now understand the step I have taken, others will be pained by it, and for this I am sorry. But I believe that in years to come more and more Catholics will look upon it as one among many necessary experimentations with priestly living. I look on the Society of Jesus with gratitude, respect, and hope for its future. A number of Jesuits have been supportive of my decision as one which may benefit the Church. Therefore, I see my past as a preparation for a new mission to which I believe myself called at this time of my life. I hope to serve the Church in the broadest sense of its mission for humanity.

8

FOR THE LOVE
OF JEANNE

by George H. Frein

Born on October 2, 1932, in St. Louis, George H. Frein
studied at Cardinal Glennon College in St. Louis, where
he received his B.A. and M.A. degrees. From his ordination in 1958 until 1965 he served as a high-school religion
teacher at Bishop Du Bourg High School in St. Louis.
During most of that time he served as chairman of the
religion department and, for two years, was chairman of
the Religion Teachers Council for the archdiocese.

In this position he was involved in improving the quality of high-school religious education. He taught a course
in catechetical theory at the major seminary and a similar
one at two of the local Catholic colleges for women. For
one year he served as diocesan vocation director. During
all the years of his service in the archdiocese, he followed
a course of studies at St. Louis University, leading to an
M.A. degree in European history.

In 1965 he was sent to Catholic University in Washington, D.C. to study in the department of religious

education. He is one of the founders of the National Association for Pastoral Renewal. On June 10, 1968, he married Jeanne Bordeau, and he and his wife are now on the faculty of the University of North Dakota. His position in the religious-studies department is underwritten by the Catholic Bishop of Fargo. He has received from Rome a dispensation from all priestly obligations, including that of celibacy.

On May 10, 1968, after ten years as a Catholic priest, I visited my archbishop, John Carberry of St. Louis, to give him my resignation from the priesthood. Very often in the past when priests left the ministry they simply disappeared. I wanted to visit the archbishop to explain to him personally, as I had told my colleagues, that I was not unhappy in the priesthood or disaffected with priestly work. On the contrary my work had always been interesting and rewarding. I had always lived with wonderful pastors and congenial associates. I had had more than my share of happiness in the priesthood. I wanted the archbishop to know that I was offering him my resignation for one reason only: I wanted to marry.

Archbishop Carberry was new to St. Louis, having been installed just one month when I went to see him. He had replaced the late Cardinal Ritter who had ordained me and had shown me a great deal of kindness and personal warmth. I did not want the new archbishop to think that I was anything but grateful to his predecessor and to the archdiocese. I especially did not want him to think that I was leaving because of any problems I had with my brother priests. The St. Louis clergy are good priests and have been very good to me. The new archbishop was fortunate to be assigned to St. Louis and I wanted to tell him so. My leaving the priesthood was simply the result of my wanting to marry.

Archbishop Carberry received me cordially and listened to me patiently. I know of a number of priests who have not been shown even simple courtesy on similar occasions. I was treated, as I had always been in the priesthood, with kindness and sympathy. The archbishop did not condemn me, but instead wanted to know about what he did not understand. He asked, "How does a priest come to think the way you do, so that he can leave the priesthood and the Church without feeling that he is doing something very wrong?"

Later when I told a friend about the archbishop's question, he said, "That was none of his business."

"No," I said. "That was a very fair question. He had eveɪy right to ask it."

It is a question that many bishops are asking themselves these days: "How can a man who has given his life completely to God come to feel that he acts honestly in leaving the priesthood to marry?" Many Catholics, and others, too, are asking themselves the same question as more and more priests seek to resign their ministry honorably—not leaving secretly as though it were a disgraceful crime.

This is a question the Church should have been asking her marrying priests centuries ago. Only *they* have the answer. If the Church wants to know why priests leave to marry, she must ask those who do.

I was happy to have the archbishop ask me that question, and I answered him as clearly and as truthfully as I knew how. I am sure that my story was not unique. Each of us tells much the same story. The individual differences serve only to dramatize the same basic fact: for some men celibacy proves to be an unrewarding experience that they are called on to change if they are to live honestly with themselves and with God. I am especially conscious of having married quite willfully and in response to what I saw to be a better life for me.

The first thing I told the archbishop was that I still saw the priesthood as a real value in the world and that it was only reluctantly that I offered him my resignation. I was not resigning because of the priesthood but because of celibacy. "For many, perhaps for most of the priests I knew," I explained, "celibacy was a liberating and rewarding experience. I know that, because they tell me and I believe them because they are honest men.

"In the seminary we were told that although celibacy was not an essential part of the priesthood, it gave priests the freedom they need to carry out their work effectively as men of God. That is true for some. It is *not* true for all and it was certainly not true for me. I believe that my negative experience of celibacy was just as real an experience for me as is the positive experience of those who are happy with it."

I was careful to explain to the archbishop that celibacy was not a disappointing experience because I did not know what I was getting into when I was ordained. There have been men who have made that claim. 1 could not plead ignorance.

Like the rest of my classmates, I was glad to be ordained. No one was happier on ordination day than I was. I freely accepted the demands of the Church requiring priests to live the single life. I had lived the celibate life before ordination and I felt that I could live it for the rest of my life. More than that, I looked forward to such a life. During college and seminary years it had given me the chance to study, free of all other cares. It gave me the time for prayer, which I enjoyed. I expected that it would provide the same sort of freedom to work long and hard for the Church, once I was admitted into the ranks of the priesthood.

After studying for so long I was glad to begin to do the work I had prepared for. I began not only freely but enthusiastically. I entered the priesthood with a large amount of idealism, but that is the way it ought to be with young priests. Their idealism is what we like about them. My own idealism was moderated enough in the matter of celibacy to make the choice realistic, I believe.

I knew that celibacy was not the same thing as the priesthood. There had been a married clergy down to medieval times. Most of the early popes, including St. Peter, had been married. There are even married priests serving the Church today, and I had met one who was a pastor in St. Louis. More than once we were told in the seminary that the Latin rite clergy was celibate in obedience to the law of the Church and not because being unmarried was demanded by the priesthood itself.

"But what if there were no such law?" I asked myself. "If the Church did not require celibacy of priests, what would they do? What would I do?" Whenever I thought about it, it always seemed to come out the same in my mind: some priests would surely choose celibacy on their own as the monks did because they saw the value of religious virginity, but most, I thought, would marry the same as the Protestant clergy marries. Whenever, in modern times, the clergy has been given the chance to marry, they have done so.

I took my suspicions to my classmates and to some of the faculty. Really I wanted to have an answer not just to an academic question but to a personal one as well. I had to admit that although I was perfectly willing to live alone in order to do the work of the priesthood, I would probably marry if the law did not forbid it.

None of those I talked to denied my suspicions. "Quite likely most priests *would* marry," they all said. One added, "So what? Priests must be celibate. You want to be a priest; you must be *willing* and able to be celibate. You don't have to *want* it for its own sake."

So I entered the priesthood with my share of idealism, but, not, I think, without having honestly and realistically faced the issue of celibacy. I was even willing to admit the wisdom of the celibacy rule. More than that, I was eager to enjoy the freedom it would give me to do the work of the priesthood totally and effectively. It seemed a worthwhile sacrifice to make. My studies had not come easily. There was no reason for me to think that success in the ministry would either. I anticipated that celibacy would offer me both the spiritual strength and the freedom needed for an effective life as a priest. It did not, but it took me a long time to admit it to myself.

Though I lived in a parish house, my major responsibility was teaching religion to youngsters in a large coeducational high school. They were a joy to teach and I threw myself into my work enthusiastically. High-schoolers grow fast, and as they grow they question everything, especially the faith of their childhood. I did not realize this at first. I had so much to teach them that I did not know that they had any questions of their own.

I spilled out my seminary education on them so fast and furiously they hardly had time to turn the pages of their books. I even prepared a book of supplementary readings for them! Only very slowly did I learn that they lived in a world every bit as real as mine and that if I were going to communicate with them, I would have to do some listening too. When I listened, I learned a lot of things about the world, about honesty, and about myself.

I remember, for example, the day—long before Vatican II was dreamed of—when we were studying about the Mass. A student asked, "Why do you say the Mass in Latin?" I explained how the Mass was the prayer of the whole universal Church and I concluded by saying, "and so the Mass is said in Latin so that it will be the same all over the world." The student's reply was so fast and honest that I could not believe it: "Yeah," he said, "that way nobody *anywhere* knows what the priest is saying!" He was right, of course, and I became a little more respectful of the adolescent mind.

When students asked, as they would from time to time, why priests do not marry, I answered as honestly as I could. I could not bring myself to say, as some books did, that celibacy made for a holier life than marriage. Nor was I really comfortable telling them that celibacy made it possible for priests to do better work. I knew that their own fathers worked at their jobs as hard and as well as I did at mine.

Yet for a long time I remained personally committed to the single life I had chosen. It continued to give me the freedom to work long hours at the high school, in the parish, and at my own continuing education. Attending classes in the evenings, on Saturdays, and during the summer, I had gained a master's degree in history at St. Louis University and had very nearly completed work for a doctorate.

One history course in particular made me reexamine my attitude toward celibacy. It was taught by a delightful Jesuit whose knowledge of the history of England was matched by a great fund of information about both Canon Law and Anglo-Saxon common law. One day when we were talking about the clergy in Tudor times he said, "You know what I think? I think that what gets put down in modern textbooks as 'the concubinage of the clergy' is really little more than medieval man's protest against the papal law of clerical celibacy."

"Medieval people," he went on to say, "were much more charitable than we are. They did not throw the priest out of his parish just because he was living with the woman who looked after the rectory. If we were as charitable as the medievals, we would probably have a 'concubinage problem,' too!"

Even I was not ready for that one. I asked, "Isn't it legitimate to demand that a priest live out the commitment to celibacy that he took on himself when he was ordained? What is so uncharitable about that?"

"Medieval people were not only more charitable," he replied, "but they were also more understanding of human nature, and so they did not insist that the parish priest do what he found to be impossible."

At the time I did not appreciate the Jesuit's answer or his insight. I had not yet found celibacy impossible. It still worked for me and I had no reason to doubt that it would continue to work.

That celibacy shortly and swiftly became a hindrance instead of a help in life and the priesthood for me was the result of my theological reeducation and my meeting and falling in love with the girl I married. The reeducation began first, but meeting Jeanne was the principal reason why celibacy got in the way of honest living for me.

Because of my interest in religious education I was sent to Catholic University in Washington, D.C. in 1962 to begin a series of summer-school courses in catechetics. Under the direction of Father Gerard S. Sloyan, the university's department of religious education had gathered together one of the best Catholic theological faculties in the country. Far from being concerned with methods of religious education, the faculty was involved in rethinking the outdated theology most of us had learned in the seminary. In place of the cut-and-dried dogma of the old textbooks they tried to create a theology that related Jesus' message to the world in a relevant and compelling way.

For me one of the most exciting aspects of these summers was the chance to think along with teachers who were trying to break new ground, even when they were talking about old ideas. Unlike the theology of the seminary in which religion seemed to belong to the realm of *things,* the new theology brought religion into the world of *persons.* God was spoken of, not so much as a Supreme Being, but as the Father of us all. Christ was not chiefly made up of two natures; he was Jesus, a person. The Church was looked upon as a community of men rather than as some sort of salvation organization. Grace was friendship with God more than a state of being or a spiritual treasure. The new theology of sin reflected a sympathy for the complexities of modern life and an open mind toward new knowledge about man that made the old moral theology with its neat do's and don'ts seem hopelessly out of touch.

I was also deeply caught up in the new liturgy that was being studied and celebrated at the university. Rather than say Mass each morning by ourselves in a little cubicle that was anything but expressive of public worship, a number of us began to attend Mass at nearby Trinity College. For the first time I began to see how the Mass, properly celebrated, could bring people together in a common worship experience.

Each summer after six weeks of study and prayer, I went home to my classroom, back to the parish and the confessional with new and fresh insights for relating the Gospel and the faith to people's lives. I had a lot to say at the end of each summer, and no doubt I many times

lectured people who had little need even for the new theology. But
more and more I listened to the questions other people had and tried
to find answers to these questions.

The more I tried to give a religious answer to the questions I was
asked, the more I came to depend upon the Jewish philosopher Martin
Buber. I read and read again his little volume *I and Thou*. It was the
best book I knew to help people see what religion was all about.

Buber's personalism confirmed what my summer-school professors
were saying. He especially brought to mind the lectures of Father
Marcel van Caster, the famous Belgian theorist. "Man-in-himself is an
unreal thing," he used to say. "No such thing exists! There is only
man-in-situation. Only man-in-relation is real, and whenever you talk
to a man you talk to one of these." To know himself, personalist think-
ers would say, man must know not just himself, but himself in relation
to the material world, in relation to others, and finally in relation to God.

This sort of thinking gave me a whole new vocabulary in which to
speak and teach. It was a whole new way of thought, and it involved
a whole new set of values. I discovered that it seemed to be a language
that people understood. Put in personalist terms the Christian religion
seemed to have new meaning for them. I was pleased and began to
enjoy my work even more.

My enjoyment did not last long. The more I followed this line of
thought and the more that I saw the Gospel in these terms, the more
uncomfortable I became. The old theology taught that the truly religious man fled from the world and from entangling personal relations
with others in order to live for God. As a result of his love for God
he may then be able to be of some help to his fellow men.

The new theology discovered and began to develop a whole set of
religious values in labor, in the material world, and engagement in
worldly occupations. Even more disturbing, the new theology questioned the possibility and the wisdom of seeking God alone. God seemed
to reveal himself to those engaged in living in close relation with
other men.

I could not agree with the theology of human relations that was
summed up in the old classic *The Imitation of Christ:* "As often as I
have been among men, I have returned less a man." Buber seemed to
me much closer to the truth when he said that we become truly ourselves only when we stand in relation to others. "I become I only by

saying Thou," he wrote. This seemed to be what Jesus meant by his insistence that we love one another. I saw no escape from the question of St. John: "How can you love God whom you do not see, if you do not love your neighbor whom you do see?"

The more I explained the Gospel in terms of the new theology, the more I became aware that I was far more isolated in the world than I ought to be or would like to be. My essential isolation began to press in on me, and I finally had to say to myself that I did not really have a truly close friend. There was no one to whom I could say "Thou" or for whom I was a special friend. I had not encouraged close friendship. I was not sure that I could.

Certainly I had parents who loved me and were very proud of my success. My brothers and sister were close, but they had their own lives and careers to follow. My family could not be expected to bear the burden of my problems in the ministry. Among my fellow priests there were a number, I told myself, with whom I had formed good friendships. But when I was honest with myself, I had to admit that they were really only colleagues with whom I shared a common pastoral and educational work. Many, perhaps most, priests have deep personal friends in the priesthood. I had to say that I did not.

The fellow priests with whom I shared my thoughts, for the most part, knew little of my inner feelings. Perhaps my reluctance to form close ties with them was due to the frequent warnings we heard in the seminary against "particular friendships." Close friendships with the laity were not encouraged, friendship with a woman seemed prohibited by celibacy, and even friendship with other priests had its own special dangers. The old ideal of holiness held out to the priest seemed to suggest that frienship with God would make true human friendship unnecessary.

When I finally realized how alone I was and how hard put I would be to name anyone as a friend, I realized that I was teaching and preaching one thing and living another. The more students and parishioners responded well to my explanation of the faith, the more uncomfortable I became. I was convinced that the Gospel message of love meant that people were to love real people and not just people in general, but I lived as though I did not need to establish an honest friendship with anyone. At times I thought it might even be impossible.

I knew that friendship was something freely given by another and could not be imposed on him by calculation. I was determined not to panic nor to build a friendship simply on my need to be honest. In any case I knew that it would be contrary to everything in my temperament and almost impossible for me to impose myself on somebody else because I was in need of a friend. I decided to be open to the possibility of friendship without doing anything to cultivate it actively.

Needless to say I had no thought of friendship with a woman, and friendship with a layman seemed nearly as unlikely since most of my contact with the laity was with young people. I expected that if I were to have a close friendship, it would have to be with another priest. It was not an especially exciting prospect. Friendship with another priest, it seemed to me, was pretty much like friendship with oneself—we were all cut from the same cloth.

I was the most surprised person one can imagine—and also one of the most frightened—when I had to say that one of my best friends was a woman. It took a little longer to confess that she was in fact my best friend and that I was in love with her.

Among the people I worked with in religious education was a Sister of St. Joseph, Sr. Ellen Terese. We had known each other and had worked together on various projects for two years before I had begun to think of her as a good friend. We had planned a number of workshops and had taught catechetical theory on a team at the seminary for two semesters. We also trained a group of lay catechists together one evening a week.

In the course of talking about our educational problems and in preparing our classes, we also began to talk about religious issues. Eventually we talked about personal concerns. Looking back on it, we did a lot of talking! Soon, even when there was no work to be done, we wanted to be together just for the sake of friendship and conversation. When I realized this, I was faced with a conscience problem.

The problem of conscience was solved in favor of the friendship. I decided not to go back on my resolution to remain open to the possibility of friendship, even though it had led to this friendship. I was conscious, from the beginning, of the problem that this raised for celibacy and I talked to Jeanne about it. She thought at first that a close relationship was possible within the religious and celibate life. I said that I was very doubtful and I was not sure that it was even desirable to force it to remain within these limits.

It soon proved to be impossible for us to keep up a close relationship if Jeanne remained in the convent. She left the order, saying merely to her superior, "I think that it is the will of God." Her dispensation from vows came within a matter of weeks.

Independently and, we thought, providentially, we were both given teaching assistantships in religious education at Catholic University in Washington. In a stroke of good luck we were free to learn where the friendship would lead without any of the inhibitions under which we had met and worked in St. Louis.

It was not long before I admitted to myself and to her that I loved her. Again we had a lot of talking to do and a lot of things to think about. First of all, I did not want to leave the priesthood and she did not want me to leave either. Since we had met, I had done better work than I had ever done before. Jeanne became my greatest encouragement and my best critic. Neither of us wanted that to end. That was on one level of thought. On another level there was a great urge to chuck the whole thing, to do what we wanted to do, and to let those who failed to understand simply make out as best they could.

That we did not follow this path was partly due to the fact that the university community proved to be very open to our relationship. Students and faculty alike knew that we were good friends and they seemed to enjoy being around us. We were invited out together to the typical round of graduate-school social affairs and entertained together in our turn. We dated freely in Washington without fear of running into people who would be scandalized by seeing us together.

Once we did bump into some of our undergraduate students at a restaurant, but they acted as though nothing was amiss and chatted with us very readily. Later when I told a collegue that Jeanne and I had run into some students while on a date, he said, "Don't worry. They will probably think there is some hope for the Church after all!"

There certainly began to be hope for me. I was loved and able to love in return. Beyond my relationship with Jeanne, there began to develop real friendships with a growing number of other people. The feeling of isolation was gone, and together we cultivated a wide circle of friends. With a number we had our theological studies in common. With others there were other interests, and with some it was just a question of enjoying one another's company.

It was a great liberation for me and it convinced me that celibacy was a mistake—at least for me. In spite of being engrossed in my studies, and as a result turned in on my own thoughts in a way I had not been since ordination, I was relating openly and honestly to others who not only accepted me but also accepted my friendship with Jeanne. I knew as well as I knew anything that the most important thing in life was not to live and die as a celibate. Being true to the love I had found was far more important, even though it was an invitation to leave the priesthood. I asked Jeanne to marry me even before I knew how it would be possible.

A few articles had appeared in the press, and journals advocating a discussion of the question of celibacy had appeared during the Vatican Council. But when the topic was brought up it was quickly withdrawn and reserved by Pope Paul for resolution by himself personally. With the topic just a little bit out in the open, we quickly came to know a small number of priests who were also in love. We met their friends and among these couples we formed many close friendships.

We began to work and to organize an effort to bring about some change in the law. We worked, knowing that no change would come in time to help us. Our time to leave would come before the ancient rule would even be modified to allow for an honorable exit. We worked at it anyway because it seemed better to do something about the future than just to bow to it. As great as our discouragements were in trying to bring the question of celibacy to the attention of the Church, they never gave me anything like the feeling of hopelessness that I had known before I met Jeanne.

Our work to provide an honorable retirement from the priesthood (at least without excommunication) for all who felt the need of it taught me all over again what I had learned from Jeanne before: celibacy could be a confining and isolating experience. It had proved to be so for many of the men we now began to meet. They gave me confidence in my own judgment and I became more deeply convinced that though celibacy may be an experience that should continue through a lifetime for some, for many others it should not.

For a long time I was somewhat embarrassed that this was the only real reason I could give for wanting to leave the priesthood or have celibacy made optional. But I now began to see that being in love with a woman was the best possible reason for wanting to leave the celibate life and that there was nothing to apologize for in that. This friendship was the most real and wonderful experience of my life, and I had no desire to do anything but live it out in marriage. There may be a true friendship in celibacy that makes life rich and rewarding and abundantly productive. I did not find it to be so, though I know others have.

Just about the time that we had succeeded in bringing the topic of clerical celibacy before the Church in this country for open discussion, Pope Paul issued his 1967 encyclical upholding the present discipline. Though I worked through that summer and the rest of the year, I was certain that I would have to leave the priesthood and accept the penalty of excommunication.

I know that Rome would never grant a dispensation on the only grounds I could honestly ask for it: I wanted to marry because I was in love. But the Church has always been good about accepting accomplished facts; perhaps I could be restored to communion with Rome later. It did not make much difference anyway because Jeanne and I never really felt we were cutting ourselves off from our Catholic families and friends. The problem was a legal one. Church lawyers could work it out later.

I now had to complete my studies and find a job. Because my degree was to be in religious studies—an overcrowded field—I was not sanguine about being able to find a job easily. I soon learned, however, that my religious standing, or lack of standing, made no difference to any of the religious-studies departments to which I wrote.

One of the schools to which I applied was the University of North Dakota. But when I learned that the religious-studies department was being funded by the churches of the state, I discounted the possibility of being accepted there. This was disappointing because Jeanne had the offer of a job there in a new educational program. The chairman of the department turned out to be a priest, Father Gerald Potter, but he too was not concerned about my personal standing with the Church.

"You are the man we want," he said, "and how you stand with the Church is not our chief concern. Our program is a strictly academic one and you will not be here representing any particular religious body. I am sure that Bishop Dworschak, who will be donating your salary to the university, will see things that way, too."

The bishop not only saw things that way but also looked upon it as a chance to offer understanding and charity in an area where he thought the Church could do better than it had been doing in the past.

We were married in June with our families and our friends congratulating us and helping us celebrate the occasion in a fitting manner.

In July we both began to teach at the University of North Dakota. When we went to see Bishop Dworschak to thank him for taking us in and enduring the consequent criticism, he received us most kindly and talked openly about his wish for a better legal process in helping priests like myself. He suggested that in writing Rome for a dispensation I keep the request as simple as possible, and he promised to write a covering letter urging that the request be granted. Before we had time to mail the letters, the bishop had a letter from Cardinal Seper, head of the Congregation for the Faith, the agency that handles these cases, asking him to contact me and have me petition for a dispensation from all my duties, including that of celibacy.

In writing to Rome, I followed the bishop's advice and kept things simple. There was hardly anything else I could do because the reason for my wanting the dispensation was simply that I wanted the Church to recognize my marriage. Again, all I could say was that I wanted to marry because I was in love. I had no other reason. It was not because I was dissatified with the priesthood or unhappy in the ministry. It was not because I did not understand what celibacy was all about when I was ordained. It was not because I was ordained against my will or better judgment. I wrote as my sole reason for asking for release from the obligation that "the experience of celibacy was spiritually unrewarding for me."

Within less than two months the dispensation was granted. Of itself the dispensation does not necessarily acknowledge the correctness of my conduct nor the correctness of my reasoning. It certainly does not validate my feelings or emotions. It simply says that Rome is willing to grant a dispensation from celibacy on this one ground alone. I left the priesthood essentially to marry because it offered me the opportunity to follow what for me seemed to me my vocation: to live and work effectively. Put more simply, I left the priesthood to marry Jeanne because I loved her.

9

LEAVING

A PRIVATE WORLD

by Joseph Blenkinsopp

Joseph Blenkinsopp was born April 3, 1927, in Durham, England. He received his B.A. degree at London University and entered upon his theological studies at the International Pontifical Atheneum in Turin, Italy, where he was ordained. He spent two years in scriptural studies at the Pontifical Biblical Institute at Rome, where he received the Licentiate in Sacred Scripture. He took his doctorate in theology at Oxford University, England.

He taught Scripture and theology at the International Theological College, Romsey, England, and at the newly established Heythrop University near Oxford. He taught Scripture at the University of Notre Dame and the Divinity School of Vanderbilt University and is currently on the faculty of Chicago Theological Seminary. Dr. Blenkinsopp has also done some archeological work in Palestine.

Along with his biblical apostolate he has engaged in lecturing and working with small groups. He is the author of *The Corinthian Mirror, a Sketchbook of Bibilical Theol-*

ogy, and of a volume entitled *Celibacy, Ministry, Church.*
He has contributed to the *Jerusalem Bible* and the *Jerome Bible Commentary* and has written numerous articles and book reviews for scriptural and theological periodicals. He is married and residing in Chicago.

Despite the many dramatic changes which have taken place in the Catholic Church over the last few years, a priest who leaves the active ministry still very easily becomes the target of criticism for whatever reasons or in whatever way he does it. All the more so if he chooses to write or speak out about it, especially if he shows the slightest self-assurance or gives the impression that he is out to capture publicity or pose as some kind of martyr. It for no other reason than this, it would be easier to take "official" advice and drop quietly out of sight. Despite all the goodwill in the world, it will be too easy to take the line that, in speaking out, he is simply rationlizing what was basically a personal spiritual breakdown.

My first reaction would be to accept the charge of rationalizing. A thin skin is no asset in this kind of situation. Besides, after the experience of the last two or three years at least, I do not need anyone to remind me how deeply and painfully personal honesty and integrity are involved in taking this step. Yet this would not justify me in accepting this invitation to engage in dialogue.

The trouble is that while the public is justifiably tired of hearing the dramatic public confessions of priests who have left the ministry, the number of those who have done so—about one thousand in the United States alone over the last two years—seems to point to a problem which needs discussing. The question is whether we are ever going to get beyond the stage of being either shocked or titillated at regular intervals and start, belatedly, to look at the problem as a whole and think about possible solutions.

Since attention generally focuses on celibacy and marriage, one remark ought to be made at the outset to help get this whole question in perspective. Responsible sources inform us that one out of five Protestant ministers leaves the active ministry every year in this country. Having worked over the past few years with quite a number of ministers ordained in their several churches, who now have no strictly pastoral ministry to speak of, I have no difficulty in accepting this. It occurred to me that I had been in this situation myself some time before I felt the need to take "official" steps toward resuming a genuinely lay status. This prompted the further reflection that I, like them, was still engaged in the ministry of teaching. This at least is a ministry witnessed to in the New Testament and listed among the "gifts" of the Spirit.

Here, as it seems to me, we come right away to the nub of the problem. As long as we think purely in terms of updating the priesthood, prescribing a more thorough training, preparing candidates more realistically to accept the burden of the celibate life, we are doomed to failure from the start. What the present critical situation calls for is a radical reappraisal of the historical priesthood *from a theological and biblical* point of view. This reappraisal, if carried out honestly and courageously, will necessarily take us behind priesthood into the wider question of Christian ministry.

It will lead us to see that the swallowing up of practically all the different possibilities of ministry into the priesthood has obscured the real meaning of Christian ministry as it took shape in the first Christian communities. This will, in its turn, force us to look again at what the Church is meant to be as a ministering community. The time for more or less *liberal* solutions, for updating and streamlining present structures, is past. What the present critical situation calls for is a *radical* solution, in the sense of a return to the roots.

In his recent book *The Priest: Celibate or Married?* Pierre Hermand says that "the Latin priesthood lives by a tradition which has never been made the object of a profound and critical examination." One of the advantages of having taken the decision to step out of the ranks is that one feels freer to ask some apparently naïve questions. Why is the form of ministry in the Catholic church today much more in line with the Old than the New Testament? Why is the priest taken to be a sacred person (if he is still unliberated from the traditional ethos) when the ministry of the early Church was so clearly nonsacral?

Is it not strange that the main qualification for pastoral ministry of the local church in the New Testament consists in being a good husband and a good father, which is precisely what disqualifies one from pastoral ministry in the Catholic Church today? Can we in all honesty dispose of these questions by loose talk about development? Does the basic *pattern* (I do not say the actual *forms*) of ministry in the apostolic Church have any relevance at all for our situation today?

A good example of the difficulty involved in asking such artless questions came to me some three years ago, when I wrote a brief article for *The Clergy Review* which tentatively argued the case for a representative not just vicarious view of Christian priesthood. The editor, who was shortly afterward to leave both the priesthood and the Church amid great publicity, accepted it enthusiastically only to write apologetically a couple of weeks later that it could not be accepted in its present form since it contradicted accepted teaching. Though no doubt prompted by the ecclesiastical censor, his reply gave me some insight into the grave *psychological* obstacles to even airing such questions for those firmly entrenched in the profession.

To bring out this important aspect of the question more clearly, I would ask the layman or parish priest to think what would have happened if he had approached a typical bishop some time before the Second Vatican Council and talked about the possibility of Mass entirely in English or celebrating the Eucharist in a private home. Yet today, no more than a decade later, both are fast becoming an essential part of the Catholic scene despite isolated pockets of resistance.

One of the most unfortunate aspects of the present situation is that so many of our leaders are frightened men who shrink from the very thought of change, the furniture of whose minds has never been dusted let alone moved in years. While not given to optimism, I would risk prophesying that within a couple of decades at the most some form of permanent ministry by married men will be just as much part of the scene as the English Mass and the house-Eucharist are now.

What I came to experience more and more, and what many in the priesthood are no doubt also experiencing, was an unresolved tension between priesthood as a cultural residue from the past and a role and function in society which made sense sociologically, that is, in terms of what I was actually doing. Having belonged to a congregation which was committed chiefly to education, I had plenty of opportunity of knowing people whose lives were spent almost exclusively in teaching subjects like chemistry and English literature, whose pastoral training and practice were practically nil and who yet were priests.

There comes to mind, to take an extreme case, a priest in Rome who had a doctorate from the Gregorian University and spent his waking hours registering Mass stipends in one of the lesser basilicas. This kind of phenomenon, with which all are familiar, has to be set over against the fact that practically all the many forms of ministry mentioned in the New Testament have been swallowed up by the priesthood.

I must add that I have also known, and still know, many priests who have found their own way, by virtue of an inner need for authenticity, to a meaningful mission and function and who are doing more good than they will ever know this side of the grave. What I cannot help noticing, however, is that in general they are available for this kind of mission and function only to the extent that they are liberated from the omnipresent mystique and ethos of priesthood.

What it amounts to, in my own case, is that for quite some time previously, I had come to realize that I was not a priest at all in the commonly accepted meaning of the term. True, it might have been different if I had been engaged significantly in pastoral work or had been responsible on a more or less permanent basis for a particular congregation or group. It seems to me that as the penumbra of the sacred dissolves, as it is doing rapidly, and as the cultural and historical factors behind the present concept of priesthood are seen more clearly, people will be asking more and more insistently why one has to be a "priest" in order to engage in any kind of meaningful ministry in the Church.

Priesthood happens wherever the reconciling, healing, and enabling power of Christ is made present. Looking back, it seems to me that the most "priestly" aspect of what I had been doing since my ordination in 1956 was not the celebration of the Eucharist, too often in private, but the opportunity afforded me to counsel people in trouble, speaking but even more listening, being human and accepting. This can and did sometimes take place in the sacrament of confession, though my own experience here would, I think, be borne out by that of many others, that the practice of regular confession now fulfills a function for which it was never intended—the periodic exorcizing of neurotic guilt. I take it as a positive sign of hope that it is now being increasingly abandoned.

In the difficulties and crises of my own life in recent years, I have always found good friends to whom I could speak openly and who could be at the same time both critical and accepting. This was especially true of the most recent crisis which led me to seek laicization. Now anyone who has gone through this will have noticed something which is so obvious that its oddity and significance might not strike him. In general, the more a person was immersed in the "official" and traditional Catholic ethos, the more difficult, if not impossible, he found it to understand, accept, share, and communicate.

I am not making any pleas, but it is surely strange that precisely in the kind of situation where the Christian "thing" should happen, so many Catholics do not have the resources to cope. Not to mention the fact that the official organs to which one has to address the petition have not even had the courtesy to reply since the petition was made twenty months ago. This is significant because a deep mutuality and communication seems to be of the essence of Christian life. However hopeful one may be, it prompts the reflection that the real Christian action is not going to take place at the center of this cultural-traditional-ethnic Catholicism but at the fringes—at least for the foreseeable future.

The priesthood in the Roman Catholic Church is one of the most rigorously organized and disciplined bodies in the world today, despite all that has happened since Vatican II. Of the Catholic priest more than of any other category of person a high degree of conformity is expected. Moreover, this expectation is still generally fulfilled unless he happens to belong to a particularly swinging group, for the most part cut off from the great mass of churchgoing Catholics unwashed by the tide of the new theology.

These expectations affect both himself and the people to whom he ministers. If he accepts and plays out the role cast for him, the result will tend to be an almost complete identification between person and *persona,* between himself as a real individual and the social image he projects. It is this identification which seems to lie behind the different personality disorders to which priests, and clerics in general, easily fall prey. But the effect on the people whose lives he influences will be even more important, though not so easy to identify and formulate. For what takes place as between priest and people is a process of mutual reinforcement.

Instead of trying to analyze what this entails, let us ask what kind of a church, better, what kind of Christian experience, we would have if the received model of priesthood were to disintegrate, which it surely will and perhaps sooner than we think. There would surely, in the first place, be less sense of guilt and more joy, openness, and freedom. Deprived of either an alibi or a moral and ritual scapegoat, the Catholic would be obliged to take over Christian responsibility for himself and his actions. No longer under the threat of supernatural sanctions, he would have to ask himself why he comes together with others to celebrate a common fellowship in the breaking of bread. More important, he would have to take coresponsibility for the life and mission of his Church.

Is this an exaggerated or idealized picture? If it is, I would only submit that it is better to exaggerate than to suppose that the situation is basically sound and all we need do is to apply the updating programs laid out in the council documents. Despite significant progress here and there we can hardly avoid the impression that there is *so much* for the sick, the weak and dying, so much isolation, irrelevance, the aridity of a plant which has been cut off near the roots and is slowly dying.

When we scan the present situation in the light of the New Testament, we can hardly avoid asking what we have made of that great hope, that possibility of new life which broke on the world nineteen hundred years ago. And the conclusion can hardly be avoided that what more than anything else has contributed to the present situation is the stranglehold which clericalism has fixed on practically every aspect of Church life. As we have seen, the priesthood has absorbed almost every form of ministry listed in the New Testament: religious orders and congregations which are meant to be charismatic are under clerical control (we even have the ludicrous spectacle of aging celibates determining what is decent for a woman-religious to wear); moral life is determined in detail by the clerical order even in those areas such as sexual relations where, presumably, they themselves have little or no experience.

A crucial case is that of the common Christian celebration, crucial since the Christian life has to be *celebrated* not *cerebrated*. Compare a typical city Mass with its anonymous and silent congregation with the kind of celebration described in the New Testament as taking place, say, at Corinth or Troas. Now at last a little joy is coming into our meetings here and there, but only at the cost of breaking with the clericalized Eucharist we have been accustomed to. Also not a little impatience.

Perhaps I could have detected a small ray of hope in a conversation overheard recently during a particularly soporific Mass in a Wisconsin

parish church. A father was admonishing, in a loud whisper, his talka-
tive little son who was about two years old. He told him to keep quiet
or he might wake up Jesus, and the child made what seemed a perfectly
reasonable reply: "People wake me up." Maybe the tide is turning
after all.

Clericalism, and in the Catholic Church this means priesthood, has
had such a preponderant influence in producing what one writer has
called "the dubious belongingness" of the present-day Christian that
we may well ask, with Bishop John A. T. Robinson, whether we are
likely to make any progress in resolving our difficulties until we have
breached the clergy-line. I do not know to what extent my own experience is representative, but it has certainly led me to the conclusion
that the priesthood, as presently structured and practiced, is largely
a sociological anachronism. This seems to be borne out, indirectly at
any rate, by responsible studies carried out over recent years, for
example those of E. Wakin and J. F. Scheuer (*The De-Romanization
of the American Catholic Church*) and Joseph H. Fichter (*America's
Forgotten Priests*). More recently the latter has stated that "the priest
who follows the book is closed to hope and involved in despair."

Some of the most perceptive people are finding forms of ministry outside of the established patterns, especially outside of the feudal parish
structure. We need the witness of these men, too. We would like them
to tell us what the tension between the new experience and the old
forms inherited from the past is doing to them. The trouble seems to be
that the understanding of priesthood as a sacred order restricted to
celibates belongs in a cultic and sacred society which existed once and
has continued residually into modern times until it is now in the last
stages of dissolution. The question is whether we can respond creatively
to the new situation today by thinking our way through cultural forms
to a genuinely Christian understanding of ministry appropriate to this
new situation.

A priest who leaves the ministry to marry walks right into the sexual
backlash which is prominent in Roman Catholicism, and to which he
himself has perhaps contributed during the time of his ministry. Not
so long ago a discerning editor remarked that it was time the marriage
of former priests was taken out of the headlines and put in the society
columns of the newspapers. While sympathizing with this view, we
ought perhaps to explain that what is happening is a process of ex-

orcism as long and painful as that of the devils of Loudon. No doubt the day will come when the Catholic will ask himself how any intelligent person could possibly have gotten himself trapped in such a dead-end; but in the meantime the only solution seems to be to go on with the talking out.

At the cruder end of the opinion-spectrum a priest who leaves the ministry to marry is thought of as simply succumbing to temptation. It would save a lot of time and energy if one could simply answer the question why one wishes to marry in the words of the Clown to the Countess in *All's Well that Ends Well:* because "my poor body, madam, requires it."

Unfortunately, however, it is never really that simple. The present discipline by which the celibate state is made the necessary precondition for ministry (even for the ministry of the young aspiring deacon) could, ideally, be accepted by a mature adult whose upbringing and environment had allowed him to overcome the disruptive aggressive and sexual drives of early years and reach the necessary degree of integration at his own tempo. This, however, is not what generally happens and it is not compatible with the blueprint for priestly training laid down in Paul's encyclical on priestly celibacy. What most priests are up against is the need to make subsequent acceptance of something that had not been the object of an antecedent specific choice. The difficulty here is that they have to contend with the accepted image of the priest. However much things have been loosened up in recent years, this image is still predominantly that of a sacred person set apart in a state of life from which, as Aquinas says, he cannot easily retire.

In keeping with this, the kind of "spirituality" officially prescribed for priests does not contemplate development on the genuinely personal level which would allow him, in a real sense, to "become what he is." Anyone who has been through seminary training will be a very lucky person if he can honestly question this. The resulting tension between a static ideal, seized on and reinforced by great numbers of the laity, and a need for genuine development, has doubtless much to do with the present crisis.

In saying what little it is possible and decent to say about the decision to marry, we have to remember that no deeply personal decision of this kind is ever entirely rational. All of one's past life with its confusions, its unresolved dilemmas, its unconscious motivation, is carried over into the moment of decision. In his recent study of clerical celibacy Schillebeecks speaks of authentic celibacy as the result of "an existential inability to do otherwise." Maybe there is something of this too at the moment when one who has been inauthentically celibate decides to marry. To suppose that marriage is going to solve all his problems would be not only foolish but irresponsible for a bachelor approaching the middle years. Yet some dilemmas can be resolved only by acting, by taking the risk and trying to live it out.

In my own experience and my observation of other people in a similar situation this question of responsibility has been uppermost. Sometimes it takes a critical situation to bring to consciousness certain ambiguities and presuppositions hidden in a situation. I am thinking here of the standard (that means *clerical*) attitude to the man-woman relationship. Though he knows he is destined for celibacy, the modern seminarian or priest feels the need for affectivity and for female company in particular.

No longer bound by the old constraints he may therefore easily be tempted to embark on personal relations of some intimacy with a woman persuaded that in so doing he will turn out to be a more mature and integrated person. Since he thinks of this relationship as on the spiritual level, or at least as a deep personal friendship, he may be surprised and worried to discover that the other person has become deeply involved, at which stage, of course, the relationship must be peremptorily broken off. The recently publicized "dating game" practiced by many Catholic seminarians illustrates not only the kind of irresponsibility which can too easily masquerade in clerical clothes but also an objection to mandatory celibacy which is too often forgotten.

To take an extreme but not irrelevant example of the same kind of irresponsibility: I have personally known priests in parish work in a Latin American country who regularly took in girls for the weekend but would not have dreamed of giving up the practice of their ministry. One of them, I recall, rationalized splendidly but was surprised when I asked about the effect of this on the Indian girls in question.

On the lighter side, we have had cases of priests retiring from the ministry and publicly announcing their intention to marry, though they have no one particularly in mind, rather like some Oriental potentate preparing to bestow his favor on one of his harem. All this throws a rather odd light on the clerical attitude to women, well documented in Mary Daly's recent study *The Church and the Second Sex*.

It seems clear not only from recent experience but from the whole history of the Church that the "gift" of celibacy is of much rarer occurrence than official pronouncements seem to presuppose. This can be seen much more clearly now that we think less and less of the Christian reality in terms of the sacred, for it is this feeling for the sacred which has underpinned clerical celibacy from the outset. Only with the phasing out of the present discipline will we be free to think again creatively of the practice of genuine celibacy, celibacy "for the kingdom of God," that is, in virtue of the revolutionary Gospel message, its embodiment and communication. Even more important, only then will we be able to think creatively about Christian ministry in the world today.

One of the most disturbing and revealing aspects of the encyclical on priestly celibacy is the assumption that a person can be conditioned or manipulated to fit painlessly into the accepted model of priestly ministry. This process, presented under the rubric of "guided liberty," is clearly meant to start at an early age when the candidate enters the junior seminary. Anyone who has had the misfortune to pass through one of these institutions (until recently the great majority of both secular and regular clergy) will probably not need to be told about the dangers and ambiguities in this concept of "guided liberty."

In my own case, I was invited to "go on" for the priesthood at the age of eleven, an invitation which I accepted, since it seemed at the time a good way of getting away from a rather unhappy home and going to a boarding school. I now see that I would have been much better advised to go to the local grammar school, but, as Kierkegaard says, though we only understand our life backward we have to live it forward. The trouble was not just that realistic sexual education of any kind was entirely absent.

This is something which can be remedied, though it may still be true, as it was a few years ago, that most candidates for ordination are first exposed to it in the last year of study, in the form of one of those little Latin manuals entitled *De Sexto*. These catalogue different forms of sexual aberration with their corresponding degree of sinfulness and are illustrated with charts of the female genitalia. Much more ominous is the creation of an atmosphere pressing in upon the young person from outside which can make it extremely difficult for him to elicit acts which are psychologically, not just "theologically," free.

Everyone interprets the "sin against the Holy Spirit" in his own way. If I, too, can claim exegetical license, I would interpret it as placing an obstacle in the way of another person's free choice. This issue is being rapidly focused and sharpened in the Catholic Church today. It was something for the council to promulgate a document on freedom, though one would not have to be cynical to note that this concerned matters over which, fortunately, the Church no longer has any control. The freedom of those in the Church over whom control in some form is still exercised is another matter. Despite the rhetoric of official pronouncements, mandatory clerical celibacy has to be seen for what it is—a violation of the free order of the *ekklesia.*

The fact that so many Catholics today are making their own decisions, in this question and in others less publicized, seems to me a very good omen. No one can grant freedom, least of all in the Christian context. It is an arduous task each one has to accomplish for himself. It is also a dangerous and ambiguous undertaking since it is so easy to pass to self-assertion, thus breaking the bond of fellowship. If we can find some way of holding together these new experiences won in faith and conviction, no matter how belatedly, by individual Catholics, we have something to draw on for the future and less reason to despair.

What seems obvious at this stage is that Catholicism in its juridical structures and its cult of the absolute is slowly and painfully dissolving. Though it is, in a way, tragic that Pope Paul should be cast in the role of a forlorn Canute commanding the waves of change to recede, it would not be presumptuous to suspect that there may be something providential in this role. Everywhere today there are to be found Catholics who, while uncertain of their "good standing," are looking for new forms of life, a new language in which to speak both to one another and to the world, new forms of community and something to celebrate in community.

Though a decision to leave religious life or the priesthood may be provoked by a purely personal crisis and will therefore to some extent be incommunicable, the frequency with which it is now happening can be understood only in this context of change and transition. This at least was clear to me from my own experience.

I would add that the difficulties, doubts, even the unfocused sense of guilt inseparable from taking this step in the case of the individual, will also be a problem for the Church as a whole during this passage from a private world with a private language into a new kind of experience, to express which we have as yet no language. The challenge of the situation, not only and not principally for the contributors to this book, is to put away fear, lay hold of our *Christian faith,* and go forward with all the courage we can muster.

People in this kind of situation tend to get a lot of unsolicited advice. From "official" quarters I have been advised to stop writing and speaking, to go somewhere where I would not be known, even to change my name. (If it had been, say, Brown or Smith this requirement might have been passed over.) Once or twice it has been suggested to me that I leave the Catholic Church. Indeed many have attempted to solve their problems by a decisive break and a new start either on their own or in another denomination.

In *Celibacy, Ministry, Church* I presented some reasons why it never occurred to me seriously to take this piece of advice. To these I would add one last point. An action is brewing in this segment of Christianity which is now unstoppable and which may well have momentous effects. I feel part of this and I want to stay with it. The day the Pope leaves, I'll leave, too.

10

MY LOVELIEST GIFT

by Peter Schaeffer

Peter Schaeffer was born May 14, 1930, in Breslau, Germany. Along with his parents and two sisters, he was forced to emigrate in 1938. The family came to America via Sweden. At the age of nineteen, Peter became a convert to the Catholic faith and, shortly afterward, entered a Benedictine monastery at Newton, New Jersey. He was ordained in 1957 and then pursued graduate studies in theology at the University of Ottawa, Canada, where he received the Licentiate in Sacred Theology, magna cum laude, ranking first in a class of thirty-six.

Refused permission to continue his studies for the doctorate, he taught German, English, mathematics, and Latin in the high school in Newton and assisted at various parishes on weekends. He was invited to serve on the faculty of St. Mary's School of Theology, Morristown, New Jersey, but was refused permission by the abbot. Instead he was sent to Namupa Seminary in East Africa, teaching Latin,

Greek, English, history, and mathematics in the high school.

He assisted parishes on weekends and conducted retreats for priests and religious of the diocese. Because of cancer he returned to the United States in May 1966. He underwent three operations and radiation treatments in the summer of 1966, which arrested the cancer. He entered on the Ph.D. degree program in German literature at Princeton University in September 1967 on a university fellowship. He was awarded a Kent Fellowship to Princeton in April 1968 and, in September of that year, married Brigitte Ehrler.

Until the very recent past, perhaps to the present day, a priest who had "left," that is, had resigned from the ministry, had thereby lost the very possibility of addressing himself to the Catholic community. Whatever he might say to explain himself was only added to his condemnation as evidence of his pride, and thus excluded, he was for all time marked with the brand of "renegade" or "traitor," his reputation destroyed, his word worthless.

If in addition, as often happened, he had—as it was crudely put— "attempted marriage," the cause of his "defection" was all too plain: he had "succumbed to the lusts of the flesh." A vocabulary was ready in advance to explain each step of the way, and the only possible expression of Christian charity toward him was to pray for his repentance.

This symposium appears to mark the beginning of a new approach to the question why priests leave, and I am grateful for the opportunity of expressing my reply to it. It is a distinctly personal reply to the question why I have left, a question which every priest must answer for himself. My reply is therefore not a closely reasoned argument, but rather the relation of experiences and the insights derived from them, and in the end, of a decision which had been long in the making.

I should like at this point to anticipate the end of the story to say that I am, in fact, married now and that my marriage was undoubtedly the final decisive step. This may not be the best technique of telling

my story or of explaining my position, but it is the only fully honest
way I know, and this is far more important to me than style of
narrative or of defense of myself. Whether without the advent into
my life of the woman to whom I am now married I would not have
come to the same conclusion I cannot say, but I can say that I could
hardly have reached it in the same way.

The point is not that here was a contrary influence to which at last
my loyalty to my ministry gave way (though some may choose to see
it thus), but that the experience of a deep human love is a process of
growth and transformation in those wellsprings of personality from
which all genuine insights take their beginning. The realization of
this experience is thus closely entwined with the events of recent
years.

A few bold strokes may serve as background, while the details will
present themselves within each later context. I was born in Germany
in 1930 of Jewish family and thus forced to emigrate from the growing
Nazi terror together with my parents and two sisters. Alone of my
family I turned to the Catholic Church when I was nineteen and
shortly after that entered a Benedictine monastery in New Jersey.

I cannot from the vantage point of the present discern my motivation then. I can only say that I considered myself entirely sincere and
was so considered by my family, with whom deeper bonds of mutual
love joined me than could be severed by even so radical a departure
from family tradition. Life was not easy in the monastery, not least
because of the regime of an abbot, since resigned, but I was so far
convinced that this was the life to which I was called that I made
religious profession and was ordained in 1957. The discerning influence
of an older priest brought it about that I was sent for further studies
to the University of Ottawa.

These were two good years, a stimulating course of studies, close
associations and friendships both in the university and in the city,
cultural opportunities, as well as occasional ministry and numerous
invitations for talks and discussions. The rector of the University
Seminary, to whom I was nominally subject, looked with disfavor upon
any social or personal contacts with the laity. But since the "proof of
the pudding" was academic achievement, the lives of the student priests
were not restricted beyond the fulfillment of this one condition. This

I fulfilled, obtaining my Licentiate in Theology, magna cum laude, and, as I was told, first in a class of thirty-six.

But the broad horizons which had seemed to appear here and even the prospect of a doctorate, from which I was at most two years away, were quickly dispelled when I returned to the monastery. Instead of a task in any way corresponding to my abilities and education, I was put into what was the abbot's chief interest—the "fund-raising" department—with a few classes of high-school German to teach on the side. This was a hard blow, but one I felt capable of absorbing, or perhaps better, one I knew no honorable way to avoid.

Yet besides the long, dreary hours typing appeal letters, filing replies, thinking up new schemes, and most of all, the incessant pressure to produce more, there were other times such as retreats on weekends, Sunday help in parishes, contacts with human situations from which I have derived invaluable experience and a few lasting friendships. After two years I was dismissed from the "fund-raising" office and at my own suggestion assigned to full-time teaching in the seminary high school. But within a year, in the summer of 1962, I was assigned, totally without any expectation, much less preparation, to the missions in East Africa. Once again I obeyed; it was at the very least a welcome change of scenery.

I spent three and a half years in East Africa, again teaching in high school—Latin, English, history, Greek, and even (completely outside my "line") mathematics—with a schedule of up to thirty class hours a week, especially heavy in the tropical climate. But I found there, perhaps not consciously until after my return to America, a kind of ecclesiastical colonialism, a vast outlay of money on mission buildings for the imposition from without of a culture, of religious forms and disciplinary requirements, completely alien to the African temperament. What was far too easily called Christianity seemed in fact to be a complex of Western European, Latin, and Italian structures, distinctly arisen out of the Counter-Reformation, and of little positive value to the African in his painful process of emergence from foreign domination.

At this point I want to mention that I had met the woman who is now my wife some time before I went to Africa; in fact, in the summer of 1959. On the basis of a very brief acquaintance several years even before that, she had appealed to me (by letter) concerning a critical personal problem. As she lived some distance away, that summer was the first opportunity after this letter to see her personally. It was, especially in retrospect, a memorable meeting, but one I can perhaps best characterize by pointing out that on Christmas 1959 I received as a present from her a set of breviaries.

I saw her twice more, briefly, in 1960 and 1961; before I left for the missions I avoided a farewell visit. But there was a regular and frequent correspondence between us from the beginning and all the years I was away. Yet she was not the only woman with whom I was on cordial personal terms. Not having been raised in a mentality overburdened with sexual fears, I was not instinctively closed to such relationships.

My return from the missions came about rather suddenly in May 1966 because of my affliction with cancer. Amid all the anxiety surrounding this fact I also felt a kind of security in being in the presence of a power higher than the designs of religious superiors. The following months were spent with three operations in hospital and radiation treatments on an out-patient basis.

Asked afterward whether I had prayed much during that time, I could only reply that I had not—certainly not in the sense of having said a lot of (or any) prayers. I was quite simply aware of the fact that just turned thirty-six, I had had a good many "good years" for which I was grateful, that I should be equally grateful if there were more to come but that I had not really any title to them. My treatments were completed by the end of August and I was pronounced out of danger.

It was just at this time that I met Brigitte again, for the first time after five years, and for the first time on a really man to woman basis. Yet as overwhelming an experience as this completely new encounter was, I still resisted its meaning and continued to do so for almost another year. It was simply beyond the grasp of my system of values, yet it was also a reality which could neither be rationalized nor labeled and dismissed. The rest of that year I was on leave, in part with my parents on a trip to Europe, in part at home with them in Washington.

In January 1967 I returned to the abbey, and distinctly felt the doors close behind me as I did. But there had been notable changes. One in particular was the only really visible change which can occur in an abbey: a new administration. The abbot, after twenty years in power, had at last realized the total futility of his regime and resigned. Since the election for a successor was inconclusive, an administrator was appointed for three years. With a view at first to teaching in a new high school connected with the abbey (which was, however, all within two years, built, dedicated, and abandoned), I was released for further studies, and was accepted with a university fellowship by Princeton University for a doctoral program in Germanic languages and literature.

But I still spent that spring and summer at the abbey, substitute-teaching and helping out on Sundays in various parishes. With the restoration of my health I also returned to a closer understanding of the current American situation and had an opportunity for extensive reading, thinking, and rethinking.

Laetare Sunday, which had unfailingly brought some distinctive joy over many years, did so again, in a new and very different way. I had never been in the habit of giving a carefully prepared sermon consisting of definite points, something which amounts rather to an instruction or a moral exhortation. Instead I had endeavored to share with the congregation the experience of the Gospel text in the immediate context of current problems, often taken from the same day's news. But this day I departed even from the thoughts that had just been circling through my mind to ponder with them the question of joy, to which this Sunday is sacred: Why is there such a frantic search for enjoyment, such a vast amusement industry, when in the end there is so little of true joy in our lives? As joy springs from love, which, when perfect, casts out fear, so it must be fear and hatred which choke out joy. Fear and hatred blind us to the monstrous spectacle of ourselves, washed, well clothed and fed, presuming to receive the Body and Blood of Christ, while that same Body and Blood of Christ, even in the least of His little ones, dirty, ragged, and starved, in Vietnam, is being torn and burned and blown to bits by *our* napalm, *our* fragmentation bombs, paid for by *our* taxes, endorsed by *our* strident nationalism.

The effect was instant. A few commended me highly for having brought the Gospel and the bitter realities of life into focus together. Others snarled the age-old rebuke "Why don't you stick to religion and stay out of politics?" at me. All this occurred on the steps of the church in a wealthy suburban parish in northern New Jersey. Within twenty-four hours the pastor had telephoned my superior and asked him not to send me to his parish again.

My superior stood firm: either I came or nobody came to help out. So in the superior interest of keeping the schedule of Mass intact, I came back for several weeks more. I preached on a variety of topics, but in the same style, and received never a word of greeting or even a mark of recognition from the parish clergy. This continued through the rest of the spring and summer, later in different parishes, but generally with the same result.

In August I preached on transfiguration, on Christian responsibility in the nuclear age, and on the following Sunday—the anniversary of the death of Franz Jägerstätter (1943), the Austrian Catholic conscientious objector—on the Christian tradition of conscientious objection. I went back to its source in Christ who had lived and died as *the* conscientious objector against the domestic, the civil, and especially the ecclesiastical structures of the time. The *Catholic Worker* picked up these two sermons and printed them in the issue of November 1967. I was, however, at once black-listed in the two parishes where I had given them.

During the summer I also gave a summer course of nine lectures to a community of about two hundred teaching Sisters on such topics as Tolerance, Christian Education, Communism (as witness to the failure of a self-righteous, complacent, uncompassionate Christendom), Woman, Conscience, War and Peace. It was received enthusiastically by most of the Sisters, including the local superior. I never received, however, the transcript of my notes (which had been promised me; I afterward published them privately under the title "It Is Now Only Dawn") nor heard from them again.

To this I could add numerous other experiences in the confessional, in counseling, within my own community, but these might only, at this point, obscure the main lines of thought I should like to present. I was aware, of course, that with respect to the average parish establishment I had committed the "unforgivable sin," stirred up controversy, encouraged independent judgment, perhaps also endangered the revenues, had, in a word, "rocked the boat." In accord with the way I understood John XXIII's famous call for "doctrinal penetration," I had ventured to break through the symbolic expression of religion to see faith rather as a constant ferment in daily attitudes.

I was fully aware of what personal consequences this had already had for me and would, with growing proportions, continue to have. But the point is: I was not afraid. This cannot be reduced to terms of courage or cowardice. I simply did not shrink from "what might happen." We have all heard it said that we should make each retreat as though it were the last one. I gave each sermon with just such a mind: to say what I was most deeply convinced needed to be said, regardless of how it might imperil my situation.

Two factors played strongly into this new sense of freedom: a sense of rebirth after my recovery from cancer (I had looked death as the utmost physical threat fairly straight in the eye, and after that, it and its lesser kinfolk held no further terror for me), and the liberating reality of Brigitte's love. Yet by the end of summer 1967, I had no idea how the fulfillment of this love and the fact of my priesthood were to come about, or indeed, if they ever would. They were simply two areas of reality to be equally borne for the time, perhaps for a lifetime.

The idea of resigning "in order to marry" was still quite outside the possibility of my thinking. The experience of years had shown me that solutions often came most unexpectedly in the thorniest problems—not by contriving, much less forcing them, but by subsequent events, by waiting and recognizing suddenly that the problem had already solved itself. This thorniest of all problems in my life was in fact solved for me within a short period of time. But here I am getting ahead of my story.

And so I came to Princeton. The academic tradition has for several generations been deeply ingrained in me by both heritage and disposition, and I do not exaggerate when I say that the return—after the vicissitudes of these past ten years—to a university campus, to books and classes, was a distinct and even physical thrill for me. But far more deeply I realized that for the first time in more years than I can recall, my mind was fully engaged, I was working to my connatural capacity. I was (the most colloquial being often the most accurate expression) "where I belonged."

I had arranged to live in the rectory of a nearby parish and to earn my living by Sunday help. My sermons were noticed almost at once— for good and for ill. The wife of a distinguished scientist here identified me as a "stranger." When I asked her why, she replied that in my sermon I had quoted Marlowe and that this simply "wasn't done" in this parish.

It was not, however, all so innocent as an occasional literary allusion,

an appeal to the imagination and the creative intellect of a congregation upon which (as indeed never upon any congregation) I simply
could not look as upon a group of stupid and wayward children. I could
not look down upon them, talk down to them, and least of all, inces-
santly badger them for money.

Perhaps I may be allowed to quote myself in the last few sermons I
gave in Princeton, for it was these that brought about the final collision.
On the last Sunday of October I said, in part: "The other indication
given us in the Gospel text is that Christ the King states as his purpose
in life to bear witness to the truth. The past generation has brought a
mountain of books around the theme of the Silent Church—far away
always in distant lands. But there is rather the Silent Church much
closer at hand whose full story remains to be written—the Silent Church
which around 1939 had not a word to say about Hitler's wars nor his
death factories, the Silent Church which around 1945 had not a word
to say about dropping atomic bombs on human beings, and the Silent
Church of this very hour. As you will recall in the ninth chapter of
Luke, Jesus rebuked James and John for wanting to call down fire on
the unbelieving cities, telling them they knew not whose spirit they had,
but when the Son of John does in fact rain down fire on those cities
which cannot bring themselves to accept his own bizarre Gospel, the
Church is once again, by and large, a Silent Church. . . . Pilate's question—what is truth?—remains hanging in the air, for *us* to answer, each
for himself."

Not long after this I was called in by the pastor of this parish, sternly
rebuked for having brought up such "controversial" questions, and
warned not to mention the war again. I could not conform to this warning, but I knew that the sands were running out.

In the middle of November I said: "Or, the Kingdom is likened to
yeast which a woman adds to a measure of flour. It has occurred to me,
perhaps to you as well, that yeast is really an altogether subversive element. But then Jesus was in his unique way also an altogether subversive person. When the dough sits, it is yeast which makes it rise. When
the dough wants to retain its shape, it is yeast which makes it take on
another. When the dough would prefer complacency, it is yeast which
'rocks the boat,' or the cooking vessel, and forces it into activity. In any
event, yeast is a disturbing factor. Hence the likeness to a subversive
element it so insistently suggests to me and perhaps to you as well."

Thereupon the pastor received a letter from a visiting college student who wrote: "But I would especially like you to know how very impressed we were by the homily which we heard at the 12:30 Mass that morning. In my thirteen years at Catholic schools I had never heard the parables so logically explained! Although the term is trite, I can find no other word for my feelings which fits better than 'inspired.' I'm not sure what priest delivered the talk, or even if it was you, but I would like him to know that he helped to make my weekend complete."

The pastor gave me this letter and for the moment seemed satisfied. I honestly think that he was not really concerned about what I said but only about favorable or adverse "public relations." It was, however, only a very temporary "stay of execution."

The showdown came after the second Sunday of December, which turned out to be my last sermon. Most cynically, as I thought, the announcements called for the administering of the Legion of Decency pledge after the Gospel, while the people were still standing, to be followed(!) by an explanation of the pledge. I did slip in, however, before the administering of the pledge that in the very text it says that it is freely made, and that accordingly everyone should feel free to take or not to take it, adding: "After all, this is a church and not a concentration camp."

This remark, springing out of the situation of the moment, had an electric effect. Afterward a few close friends, including one of my professors, who were present, told me that they knew that this would be "the end" for me in this parish. I went on to say that the problem of decency seems to turn not so much about topless dresses as topless people, those who had their heads blown off by our murderous weapons; that the deeper obscenity lay not in undraped bodies, but in starved, charred, desecrated bodies; that the promotion of decent books, films, television programs, had first of all to take notice of the constant flood of violence, of vindictiveness, of hatred, inundating our homes unchecked and even endorsed. If we were earnest in loving our neighbor as ourselves, and indeed, of loving our enemy and doing good to him—the one great precept of the Gospel—then for every Vietcong soldier killed we should have as copious tears to shed as if it were our own mother. Instead we triumph over the growing statistics of enemy dead. I do not claim that I have such tears to shed, but it disturbs me that I do not.

It is useless afterward to wonder whether I could or should not have expressed myself differently. There is no other solution to the perennial tension between the security of the speaker and the freedom of his word except that born out of the crisis of the moment. But to calculate in advance and to withdraw all manner of expression which could possibly give offense is not my idea of a Christian sermon. I could not function this way even if I had had a mind to do so.

Again there were letters. The wife of a prominent local psychiatrist wrote: "How can we thank you for your beautiful sermon this morning? Before you had finished the announcements, we knew that you were very special. . . ."

Another mother wrote: "It has inspired me to take the time from the care of four small children to write you. It has stirred up thoughts which have remained undisturbed too long. It has renewed my faith. My Lord, if there were only more men like you!"

But it was too late now; the pastor had summarily forbidden me ever to preach again, and while I was not asked to leave the rectory, I felt I had no choice but to do so. Whatever else I have been called in canine terms, I am not the sort of dog who can agree to bark no more in exchange for free room and board.

Accordingly I took my leave, removed to the graduate college of the university, and informed my superior as well as the local bishop of what had taken place. My superior expressed his understanding. The bishop, despite three letters addressed to him over the next several months, did not reply with a single word.

Into this sufficiently dramatic week fell another event of deepest significance to me. My best and oldest friend at the abbey, a priest ten years my senior, who had also been my confessor for the past eighteen years (except for the time I was in Africa), suddenly died at the age of forty-seven. In the thirteen years following a serious accident, during which he had received totally inadequate medical care, he had suffered constantly and intensely.

After an enormously complicated operation the previous year he had just begun to recover a little, when one morning he was found in bed dead, the core of his strength evidently sapped to the dregs. Yet he had always been the kindest, the warmest, the most understanding of men, universally loved and respected within and without the community, even by those who had had only the slightest acquaintance but had received a lasting impression.

Related to him by innumerable bonds of friendship and affection, affinity of thought and taste, shared memories and kindred dreams, I had confided my inmost hopes to him just before his death, and received his blessing upon them. I attended his funeral and felt a realization at once unsummoned and irrefutable that in burying him I had also buried much of myself, my past, and my ties with the life we had shared. The Christian mystery and the mystery of the individual Christian can, after all, be ultimately expressed only in terms of life and death and resurrection, not those of Canon Law, of obligations and dispensations.

I spent Christmas with my family in Washington and the remainder of the Christmas holiday with Brigitte. The spring, the season sacred to the germination of new life, brought with it an opportunity for reflection upon all that had taken place. My academic work, equally enjoyable, demanding, and so far successful, received the recognition of a Kent Fellowship from the Danforth Foundation, enabling me to continue my studies to the Ph.D. There were petty harassments from the parish in which I had lived (and to which I had carefully given my forwarding address), such as the suppression of mail, telephone calls, and the information given out that "I was no longer a priest," long before I had reached any certainty on this point within myself, much less afforded any external evidence for such a conclusion. These did not, I think, fall too heavily into the balance.

I was not even under constraint to return to the religious community, where I saw more clearly than ever that I should simply be buried alive and invite an interior catastrophe. I had been expelled from only one parish and treated as nonexistent by one bishop. But what had occurred there was bound to repeat itself. I could no longer work within a moral system which still, to the present day, condemns a man for all eternity for the willful missing of a Sunday Mass but cannot bring itself to condemn as absolutely ABC warfare. It afflicts millions with mortal guilt over one "impure thought" but allows to run unchecked thoughts, plans, and massive actions of vengeance, violence, and hatred. It displays a system of symbols and laws but shuns a confrontation with the meanings contained in them. It fosters a neurosis of fearful anxiety for individual salvation and looks askance at a world to be saved.

The question of celibacy is most important at this point, though it is far from the only immediately personal question. To what extent my thinking was and is shaped by a "need" to rationalize its obligation, I am not the person to say. My purpose here is not to justify my story, but only to tell it. If, as a future brighter day may bring about, there were no conflicting opposition between marriage and ministry, there would have been no question to answer. But as it is, there is such a question and the answer was ultimately shaped by this reality: that Brigitte is the greatest, fullest, loveliest gift I have ever received from above, and that it is a gift offered and meant to be accepted gratefully and with full responsibility.

One of my sisters had often joked with me that it was just as well I would not marry, because there was simply no woman who could possibly fulfill all my expectations in terms of character, education, refinement, taste, and temperament. But Brigitte has fulfilled and surpassed them. If beyond the innumerable I should try to pinpoint wherein she was so very different from every woman I had previously encountered, it would be in this: she never asked but always gave; she never demanded a decision but waited quietly, patiently, serenely, to see if perhaps it might somehow come of its own accord. She never imposed herself but was always "there"; that force which is greater than any force, commonly called a Loving Presence. We were married on the fourth of September in 1968.

It is not my purpose to ask for a dispensation and/or permission to marry. For this I shall not try to give a dogmatic but only a personal explanation. I do not feel that a rubber stamp of an official upon a form, on which I am to him no more than just a name together with a formally expressed set of circumstances, could possibly have any bearing upon the reality of our lives, nor that it would have anything particularly sacramental about it.

Besides, it would make a mockery of a permission to ask for it in circumstances in which it could not possibly be given. Brigitte was previously married and divorced, and I know Canon Law well enough to realize that there is not the slightest possibility of this former marriage, to which no further reality attaches than a canonically legal one, ever being annulled. Truly it is written, "What God has joined together, let no man put asunder," but the question remains, "What *has* God indeed joined together?" I am convinced that the answer cannot be found solely in the accumulations of centuries of ecclesiastical jurisprudence whose end product is often too facilely presented as "divine law" to the complete exclusion of a Living God manifested in living realities.

Nor do I intend to ask for what is rather unpleasantly called a "reduction to the lay state." (I may, of course, be so reduced just the same, but I do not intend to ask for it.) I have never considered myself as exalted above the lay state, so that there is in my mind no need now to be reduced to it. That the concept of the "lay state" derives from a feudal and not an evangelical understanding is a question I need not further discuss here.

Perhaps I am thus looked upon as having left the Church as well as the priesthood. It does not seem so to me, for my understanding of the Church was never that of a club one joins or leaves. Membership in the Church is a symbolic expression of the fact that a man acknowledges himself beyond himself to belong to the Family of Man. Hence leaving the Church could come about only by the repudiation of this communal bond, which is not my position at all.

As for the priesthood, there seems to be in the idea of a "priest forever" not only a threat but a promise. I never, not even from the beginning, looked upon the priesthood as primarily concerned with the performance of ecclesiastical functions, but with eating and drinking, with speaking hope and comfort, with "being there," accessible and dedicated to others. And this concern is not annulled, but abides to find expression in new forms.

One last thought. A question which has been put to me more than once recently, and most urgently by someone particularly dear to me: "What about us whom you leave behind?" I cannot pretend that my personal ministry had ever such a wide influence as to leave anyone deserted now. Those few whom I really felt I had "reached" (whether in the confessional, from the pulpit, or elsewhere) were also the ones who least needed it. They had already reached in mysterious ways the very point at which I was able to "reach" them. And I wish always to be and to remain available to those who feel that I have in any way anything to offer them.

I have no quarrel with anyone, no score to settle, no resentments, but rather gratitude to all those in smaller and larger circles who have in any way enriched my life and perhaps enabled me to enrich theirs. The story I have attempted to relate must serve as its own explanation. With apologies to the famous author whom I am hereby paraphrasing, I might conclude by saying: For those who understand, no explanation is necessary; for those who do not, none is possible.

11

WHY PRIESTS MARRY

by William J. Sullivan

William J. Sullivan was born on May 10, 1931, in Arlington, Massachusetts. He entered the Society of St. Paul and studied at St. Paul's College, Washington, D.C., where he received the B.A. and M.A. degrees. On May 11, 1957, he was ordained at the Church of St. Paul the Apostle in New York. His first full-time assignment as a priest was to the Newman Center at the University of California in Berkeley.

While there, he also pursued graduate studies in philosophy. From 1960 to 1962 Father Sullivan served as treasurer of the National Newman Chaplains Association. In 1961 he was assigned to the Newman Center at the Massachusetts Institute of Technology in Cambridge. In August 1962 he was sent to Paris to complete his doctoral studies in theology at the Institut Catholique. While in Paris he resided at the rectory of the parish of St. Severin and participated actively in all the work of the parish and served as chaplain for the youth of the parish, both French and foreign born.

In May 1963 he received the Licentiate in Sacred Theology from the Institut Oecuménique in Bossey near Geneva, Switzerland. This institute is under the joint direction of the World Council of Churches and the University of Geneva. He received the certificate of completion in January and then began field work in the offices of the Faith and Order Secretariat in Geneva at that time. He defended his thesis at the Institut Catholique on May 25, 1967, and received the doctorate in sacred theology with honors.

He resigned from the Paulist community and received from Rome a dispensation from celibacy. He is married to a French girl, Jeanne Verliac, and is working for the Office of Economic Opportunity in Washington, D.C., as a program specialist in the Job Corps.

The old answers to the question why priests marry were quite simple. I remember dismissing the question casually by explaining that such priests must have got mixed up either mentally or morally. No one ever corrected this notion in my hearing. And it was only when I became a married priest that I realized how grossly unfair my answer had been.

Such an answer may still be heard. But fewer people are likely to take it seriously today. Dramatic changes are taking place. An older priest, one of my former seminary professors, recently came to dinner at our apartment. After a delightful evening, he told us both, "I had to come to tell you 'God bless you both.'"

In the long history of clerical celibacy, married priests have never been so well considered. And now we have the opportunity to explain why we have married. I can write only for myself. Other married couples will immediately understand the impossibility of generalizing about an experience which is common to so many and yet unique for each.

Priests marry because they are men. Married priests are neither angels nor villains. St. Paul understood that men pledged to the service of the Church would want to marry. And he counseled them to do so even though he wished that all men were as he was (I Cor. 7:8–9). Now celibacy has become compulsory for men who are called to the priesthood in the Latin rite Church. And Catholics have become accustomed to their priests being bachelor Fathers.

In a small French village some fifty miles south of Paris, I embarrassed a French couple when I asked why the man of the house could not take the place of the village priest. I did not ask the question in jest. It was very real for me and even more so for the diocese which was pitifully understaffed. The village priest whom I had replaced for two weeks was also responsible for four other villages.

The husband and wife looked at each other and blushed before the wife finally managed to say, "But we are married . . . he is my husband."

I tried again. "What difference does that make? Your husband is a good man."

This time there was no hesitation. "Father," she said, "you do not understand."

And she was right in a way. I still do not understand how a man united in marriage with a woman can, in their one flesh, become a sign of Christ and the Church (Eph. 5:21ff.) and at the same time become unworthy to help fulfill the commission Christ gave to his apostles.

I asked the bishop of this same diocese if he would be in favor of ordaining married men to resolve his vocation crisis. His response was hesitant but positive. "We are not yet ready to do that, Father. But it will come." At that time, Vatican II had not yet given its permission for married men to be ordained to the diaconate.

In the course of his ministry, a priest meets hundreds and even thousands of women. With some he is a Father or a brother. With others he is able to relax and enjoy being a man. For most priests, the male-female relationship never goes any further than that. Married priests remain in the minority.

A retreat master once warned us seminarians about the danger of casual friendships with women. "It may start with a quiet drink together after sodality," he said, "but it's likely to end in bed." He explained to us that priests who married had been careless about the grace of the priesthood. And undoubtedly some priests are married because of one wild passionate night. Perhaps some priests do marry with a shotgun at their backs. But others do not.

My marriage was as free and as joyful as the love Jeanne and I had for each other. I met my wife in a youth group in Paris. She was an active participant in that group; I was its newly appointed chaplain. She was also a beautiful and stimulating young lady. She is the only true answer to the question why I married.

Two of my best friends in the priesthood had already warned me that I would have trouble as a priest because I permitted myself to become involved in the lives and problems of other people. They chided me about going to private apartments. And yet they knew that I did not go to drink or to sleep but to counsel people who needed desperately what only a priest can give. These priests told me I would have been better advised to refer such people to a policeman, a doctor, or a lawyer.

And some priests are able to carry on their ministry in this way. They avoid all involvement by referring people to specialists. And even though their intentions are excellent, the yellow pages of the telephone directory could easily replace them.

I did not marry because I became too involved with a woman and her problems. I married because I was in love with a woman who rounded off my edges and squared my corners. We became involved with each other because we were both involved with Jesus Christ. We worked together in a busy Parisian parish to give men and women, who had nothing, a bite to eat and a chance at a job. We both had other full-time responsibilities.

I was a graduate student at the Catholic University of Paris. She was a technical assistant for a French doctor who was doing research into the causes and possible cure of cancer. We both worked for a common cause and gradually grew into a single flesh.

Once we had both realized and told each other that we were in love, we talked long and hard about what to do. We could not simply forget each other. Jeanne suggested that she enter a convent. And the idea had a certain superficial appeal. We talked of saints Francis and Claire, John and Thérèse, and Francis and Jeanne and imagined ourselves as their twentieth-century successors. But finally we rejected the idea. Jeanne had no desire to serve God as a nun, and the last thing I wanted was for her to enter a convent.

Then we began to ask each other and others hard questions about why priests do not marry. We knew the standard answers about the priest being consecrated to God alone. They no longer rang true. Jeanne was not in competition with God. Our love for each other had intensified our love for God and increased my efficiency as a priest.

Jeanne wanted me to explain the real reason why priests do not marry. She respected my vocation but insisted that both of us must understand why I was forbidden to marry. We both knew that marriage would automatically terminate my services as a priest. The Church tolerates alcoholic and immoral priests. Ineffective and stupid priests are allowed to continue their ministries. The law eliminates only those priests who marry. And both of us considered the law absurd for these reasons and unjust for so many others.

The law of celibacy did not forbid us to work together in a common cause. The law did not compel me to live within an all-male society. Because the law permitted me to be with women, to work and pray with them as well as with men, it seemed unreal for the law to specify that I should not fall in love. Unless the priest is able to give himself totally to God and share the presence of God with others without committing himself to any other person, it is impossible for him to remain celibate.

We both recognized and respected the real meaning of celibacy for a man who lives in a monastery. He lives for God alone. He has no other concern than to deepen the life of the Lord within himself.

In a sense, the monk is indifferent to other people and their reactions. His share in the mission of the Church is to assure that in his own person and in the person of his own religious community, the unity between God and man is as intense as the Son of God has made possible by the incarnation. The monk focuses upon the world beyond time in which God and man will be united without end. And, insofar as he is a good monk, his only involvement is with God. He may bake bread that is world famous, or win prizes with his cattle or his wine. But the real reason he bakes bread, raises cattle, or makes wine is that the combined consciousness of the monastic movement appears to have discovered that occupations such as these free a man to give himself more completely to God. His only real concern is to live as many as possible of his twenty-four hours each day in conscious awareness of God's presence.

Jeanne and I knew full well that I had no such vocation.

My daily Mass, office, rosary, and whatever other prayers I found

time to offer each day were the source for all that I was able to do. As
I became one with her in Jesus Christ, both of us together conscious of
our unity in Christ were better able to do our thing as the Mystical
Body in that place. I as a priest and she and every other member of that
community sought to grow closer to Christ so as to carry out more effectively our share of the mission of Christ as a team. In such a situation,
it was impossible to grow in Christ without growing into and with
others.

Our particular team had already produced two engaged couples.
Jeanne asked why I had been so pleased at the engagements of these
people and so hesitant about the possibility of following in their footsteps.

Producing good Catholic marriages had always been a praiseworthy
goal for a Catholic club. Some had no other goal. But I had never
thought before that the priest might also get married.

And that was the rub. Jeanne could not believe that there was something unique about the priest which prevented him from getting married. One day she said to me, "You have walked and talked with me.
You have eaten and drunk with me. The only thing we have not done
together, and the one thing you insist is forbidden, is to marry and live
together as husband and wife. Is it because the Church believes deep
down that something is really wrong with sex?"

She knew the answer. But the question had to be asked. Marriage is
a sacrament instituted by Christ. And the married couple is a sacramental. The one flesh of a husband and wife is a real sign of the unity
between Christ and the Church. Because marriage is sacred, it was impossible to explain why the Church, by law, forbade priests to marry.
Marriage could not be sacred for everyone except priests.

"How could you encourage Claude and Françoise to marry," she
asked, "if it was not something beautiful and good?" The only reason
I could give why marriage was sacred for everyone except priests was
that the law of celibacy forbade priests to marry.

My argument was hopelessly circular. Marriage for priests was wrong
because the law forbade it. And the law forbade it because it was
wrong!

Marriage has made some priests pass through a severe crisis of conscience. Some never overcome their feelings of guilt. I never believed
that the law could make something evil out of our marriage. My experi-

ences on the staff of a Parisian parish had taught me to look beyond the letter of the law to its real meaning.

The church at which I served had been severely criticized for its liturgical innovations. The cardinal archbishop of Paris publicly censured the parish when it introduced the custom of saying "This is the Body of Christ" at Communion. I was privileged to share their joy when Vatican II endorsed many of their principles and cleared the way for the introduction of many of their innovations into the liturgical life of the universal Church. And, in my own small way, I worked with them to advance this cause of liturgical reform.

One evening, I offered Mass for a community which was composed, for the most part, of the homeless who lived and begged on the streets of the Latin Quarter. They had been my parishioners for two years.

Before the Mass, a member of our youth group suggested that I celebrate the Mass entirely in French. The Church had not yet introduced the vernacular into the Canon of the Mass. And some commentators insisted that the words of the Canon were too sacred and their meaning too important to be pronounced in any language other than Latin. An ancient law was the only real authority for this view.

During the short sermon I had a chance to look around and see who was in the congregation. Many were alcoholics just sober enough to participate at this Mass. Many of them had not entered a church since childhood, except to beg or to steal. All of them were men and women with whom I was on a first-name basis. It struck me how bizarre it would be for an American who had learned French to converse with them on the street to break into Latin at the Offertory of the Mass. And so I motioned for a French missal and celebrated the rest of the Mass aloud and in French. What is now common practice in every French-speaking diocese in the world was then forbidden by universal Church law.

No one at that Mass knew enough about the law of the Church to be scandalized. However, I let the pastor know as soon as possible what I had done. His reaction was typical of his attitude toward the mission of the Church. "But of course," he said, "it would have been unpardonable to have celebrated that Mass in Latin."

To my knowledge, no other Mass had been celebrated in the vernacular in that parish up to that time. However, the very next day, the priests decided that the Mass for the children of the parish would be entirely in French every Sunday. They believed it was more important for the young boys and girls of the parish to grasp the Word of God in their own tongue than for them to obey even a universal law.

Casual lawbreaking was not the name of this game. I tried to understand and conscientiously obey the law of celibacy in exactly the same way that they understood and obeyed the liturgical laws.

The almost constant problems the Church has faced in enforcing this legislation made me suspect that the real meaning of celibacy has never really been understood. Of course, everyone believes he understands that celibacy excludes marriage. But the real meaning of celibacy has to be more profound than that. It is unbelievable that the Holy Spirit would confuse the Church with such a triviality. And yet, the one, clean-cut, irreversible violation of celibacy is marriage.

Celibacy as it is lived and understood by monastic communities is more profound. But we should not forget that the life of an average monk resembles only superficially the life of the active priest.

Celibate monks are not busy organizing black commandos. Active priests may see no other way to preach Christ. Celibate monks are withdrawn in monastic cells. Active priests march in Atlanta and demonstrate in Washington for their confreres. Neither the priest nor the monk marries. But very devout celibate monks have insisted, in my presence, that if marriage would help them to love God, they would marry.

Life in Christ is the major focus in life for such men. Habits, language, and customs are only accessories which should help to bring them into a more profound intimacy with the Lord. And the absence of women from the monasteries of male religious is only a custom, albeit a very ancient one. However, the monastic movement could shrug off even this custom. And one reason is that celibacy is a commitment to God and not a refusal of the female sex. Celibacy, as the monk understands it, is a refusal of any alliance with any person, place, or thing that would deter him from intimacy with the Lord.

I do not pretend to have an exhaustive explanation of what celibacy demands of a man. I am certain it means more than not marrying a woman and suspect that it may not mean that at all.

Celibacy does certainly oblige a priest to a total dedication to God. But marriage does not interfere with that. Celibacy certainly obliges a priest to love all men in Christ without any exceptions. But marriage does not interfere with that. Celibacy certainly obliges a man to be ready to give up everything he has for the love of God. But marriage does not interfere with that.

Celibacy has been popularly defined in negative terms for so long that most people know only that celibates are not married. Celibacy, as I understand it, is the priest's pledge to the Church to fulfill his share of the mission in complete dependence upon Christ. Celibacy is also the Church's guarantee that it will back up and support its priests in every way so long as they remain faithful to their pledge. Celibacy imposes reciprocal obligations.

This interpretation is sufficiently vague to liberate celibacy from any narrow identification with the prohibition of marriage. Such an approach to celibacy makes the law more meaningful identifying it more closely with the virtue of charity. In this light, celibacy becomes a positive commitment to life and love that modern men can understand and make. Such an approach makes it easier for this priest to believe that the Holy Spirit guided the Church to legislate celibacy, and it could help the Church to evolve a more adequate and precise understanding of what celibacy really means.

I have talked at length with other priests about celibacy. What priests themselves understand by celibacy is of capital importance if we are ever to understand what celibacy really means.

One priest told me he was celibate because he had given his word and felt obliged to honor his commitment. It's the honorable thing to do, he said. His answer still does not satisfy me because honor is far more complex than giving one's word. A man must understand what he has given his word to do. If that priest should ever fall in love, he may well understand the demands of honor in another light. But, even more important, the law of celibacy can only compel the obedience of an honorable man if it can be interpreted in a reasonable way. Honor does not smother reason.

No priest ever told me that he thought bachelorhood was essential to maintain his continuing relationship with Christ. No priest ever told me that he feared female companionship would exclude the grace of Christ from his soul. One priest did tell me that celibacy would pose little or no difficulty if priests would take adequate recreation with their fellow priests. He suggested at least two afternoons each week on the golf course.

Finally one priest admitted, "I am not married because I have not yet

met the woman I love. If I should meet and fall in love with a woman
whom I believe should be my wife and the mother of my children, I
would marry her if she would have me." He added, "Until that day, I
am and will remain celibate. Who knows? I may even die a celibate."
This man is still a celibate priest.

These words could be shocking to Roman Catholics who have grown
accustomed to the law of celibacy. St. Paul would not raise an eyebrow
at them. He advised celibates of his own day to take much the same
attitude.

In discussing why priests marry, we cannot forget that married love
is always a gift of God. My wife and I were born four thousand miles
and eight years apart. If God had not called me to the priesthood in the
Paulist Fathers, we never would have met. Some may be unwilling to
believe that God is ever responsible for a priest's marriage. And yet we
administered the sacrament of matrimony to each other in a quiet
church in the presence of another Roman Catholic priest delegated by
the bishop to be the official witness of the Church.

This means that priests marry because they respond to the grace of
God. And it means also that some priests who do not marry may well
have refused that grace. The refusal of love is always a refusal of God.

Of course it is also possible that the priest who refuses to marry does
not act out of fear or self-respect. His concern is neither to protect himself nor to preserve a good reputation. He could honestly feel that commitment to another person would make it impossible for him to love
God.

Such high motives are not always found in those priests who refuse
marriage. One priest asked me to arrange with his religious community
for money to be sent each month to a woman whom he had made preg-
nant. He wanted an intermediary to protect his good name within the
community and to assure that no reprisals would be made. He expressed
no emotion for the woman, had no intention of sharing her pregnancy,
and showed no concern for his unborn child.

I refused to act as intermediary for this man. I cannot believe that
what he wanted to do is what the Church means by guarding one's
celibacy.

Jeanne proposed one day that she would go away and leave me.
"You cannot leave because you are a priest," she said. "It is only
normal that I should go." She had no idea where she was going or

how she would live once her voyage was complete. "What difference does all that make," she asked. "I will go somewhere too far away for you to visit me. Then you will be free to forget me and to continue your life as a priest." I refused to talk about such an absurd solution.

The idea repulsed me. Christianity made human sacrifice outmoded. We Christians still smile with superiority when we think of how pagan religions sacrificed virgins on fiery altars. I had no right to ask Jeanne, and no intention of permitting her, to sacrifice her life so that I could obey a law which neither of us understood. And yet one priest chided me for not accepting her suggestion. "It would have been the perfect solution," he told me. I do not believe that any interpretation of celibacy which excludes charity can possibly be Christian.

I do not know why all priests do not marry. I have shared with you some of the reasons I have heard why priests do not marry. I do not know either if some of the reasons why I married would be the same for other priests.

I had never met a married priest prior to our marriage. Since that day, Jeanne and I count from twelve to fifteen among our friends and acquaintances. All of them were functioning as priests two years ago. Almost without exception, they were married in civil ceremonies. Some are still waiting for a response from Rome to their request for dispensation from the obligation of celibacy. None of them has lost the faith. Some have become bitter.

They would have wished that their marriages had been blessed by the Church in which they had labored so long as priests. Some wanted this so badly that they arranged for an underground ceremony to be performed by a fellow priest. I do not believe such a ceremony has any real meaning because the celebrant is not and cannot be the official witness of the Church. And yet I understand the emotional need that some men have felt for such a ceremony.

The law forbade them to marry. And their consciences compelled them to violate the law. In its Declaration on Religious Liberty, the Second Vatican Council teaches that a man is not to be forced to act against his own conscience. And yet the way in which Church law is currently enforced makes it practically impossible for a priest to marry within the Church and thus forces him to a civil ceremony outside of the Church.

The married priest can confess sorrow that the laws of his Church prevented him from marrying within it. I could not confess sorrow that I was married. Neither my wife nor I stopped receiving the sacraments. Our pastor was aware of our canonical status and never cautioned us not to receive them.

Most priests are sufficiently well instructed to know that Church law can never compel them to act against their consciences. The American bishops recently pointed out, in a totally different context, that a man is certainly not to be forced to act against his conscience "in any conflict between a practical dictate of conscience and a legislative or administrative decree of any superior." However, so long as the law of celibacy remains unchanged, the priests who choose to disobey it cannot do all they believe conscience demands. Reform is essential.

The current interpretation of celibacy causes suffering not only for the priest and his wife but for other members of the couple's family as well. It gives rise to scandal because priests are not permitted to marry and yet they do marry. Current interpretation of celibacy also results in the priest's being excluded from his ministry when he marries. And beyond doubt, the mission of the Church suffers from each of these factors and the total of them all.

As serious and perhaps even more serious than all of the aforementioned consequences is that current disregard for the law of celibacy could bring the charism of celibacy into disrepute. Celibate love like married love cannot be legislated. The Church has established forms within which the charism of celibacy may be lived and fostered. But the presence of so many married priests inevitably casts doubts upon the commitment of all celibates. These doubts can only be lifted if the bishops have the courage to abolish the law because of their concern for the charism.

There is also a positive side of this movement of priests toward matrimony. A new ministry is being born. The rectory and the full-time priestly staff are gradually being phased out. Married priests, even though they lack any episcopal mandate to perform priestly functions, are the counterparts of the priest-workers in Europe.

We are not hemmed in by rectory walls or strange garb. We work eight hours a day, side by side with other men and women. And we are called upon to put our Christian principles into practice in the ambiguous situations of the working world instead of in the safe confines of the pulpit.

Jeanne and I did not marry to reform the Church or to change its ministry. We married because we loved each other and dared believe that God was the source of that love. And we still believe that what God has wrought is wonderful beyond words.

12

A PRIEST
WHO DIDN'T LEAVE

by Carl J. Hemmer

Carl J. Hemmer was born in Syracuse, New York, on March 7, 1932. At the age of nineteen, he entered the Society of Jesus and studied at St. Louis University where he received the B.A., Ph.L., and M.A. degrees.

He later studied theology at Woodstock College, Woodstock, Maryland, and received the Licentiate in Sacred Theology degree. During his final year of theology at Woodstock, he engaged in many forms of priestly ministry in the mission parishes of southern Maryland. With other Jesuits he worked closely with the men of the Washington Professional Sodality. He also served as executive secretary of a pioneer leadership program for Catholic African students in the United States.

In Mexico he served in several parishes and ministered to various student groups. In Madrid, Spain, he ministered in a parish for poor migrants and as an assistant to United States military chaplains. On returning to the United States in 1964 Father Hemmer continued extensive weekend parish work while pursuing doctoral studies at Columbia University. In December 1967 he withdrew from the Society of Jesus and applied to Rome for dispensation from celibacy. After successive letters went unanswered over a period of more than five months, he married Patricia Harris on June 15, 1968, in the chapel at Columbia University.

Carl Hemmer was one of the founders of the National
Association for Pastoral Renewal and is continuing his
studies for the Ph.D. degree at Columbia University.

It was the most painful November day I've ever spent. I had flown
home that day, a short year ago, to officiate at the baptism of my sister's
latest child. But I had another purpose for that trip: it was to be the
time when I would tell my mother and my family of my plans to marry
and thus to lose my right to function as a priest. I told them, as simply
as I could, of my plans and the reasons for them, but no words could
make that day less painful for us all.

How does a priest tell his loved ones that he is "leaving"—tell them,
I mean, in such a way so that they understand he is not betraying his
priesthood or their best hopes for him? It would have been far easier
if I had decided that the priesthood was not for me or that I no longer
believed as a Catholic. They would have been shocked and saddened,
but they would have understood my words.

It was so much harder to reassure them that I intended to remain a
priest even though the Church's rules would soon tell them that I had
left. No seminary training of mine ever dealt squarely with the problem
of Catholics who are unjustly rejected by Church authorities; no
pamphlet from the parish church ever taught them what to think "When
Father Leaves."

A flood of emotion inevitably choked off my family's initial effort to
understand my decision. I could not explain why I was making such a
drastic choice without attacking (charitably, I hope) some of their
most cherished ideas of what the Church is and what a priest must be.
How could I convince them that I had not simply let an infatuation
run away with me, that I was not hypnotized by some romantic notion
of married life, that I would not be making the decision at all if I
didn't really want to be a priest? There was so much to say, so much
discussion needed of our normally unexamined Catholic beliefs about
priesthood and marriage, so much, much more than one November day
could hold without pain.

My decision to marry was, in no way, made in haste. It was nearly
two years earlier when I first began to think of celibacy as an issue

that pertained to me. I was then a Jesuit graduate student at Columbia University. I had been ordained in 1962 and was as active in priestly work as my studies would permit. In the winter of 1965–66 celibacy became a topic of increasing interest among American Catholics. Initially, my feelings were those of the detached observer. As a religious for fifteen years, I had learned to see the advantages of the dedicated single life, and as far as I was concerned, my choice of the unmarried state was not up for review.

However, I was keenly aware of the difference between the stimulating community setting in which a Jesuit like myself freely chose to live as a single man and the antisocial atmosphere of many rectories in which parish priests had to endure their imposed celibacy. My theological training helped me to evaluate the intricate reasoning that was supposed to justify the practically inseparable bond tying priesthood to celibacy in the Latin rite. It took little effort to see that optional celibacy had to come if the Church was really intent on a renewal springing from a fresh awareness of and fidelity to the diverse graces with which the Spirit of Jesus makes her live.

At this stage I was still "uninvolved"; I was not dating anyone and, in fact, had no desire to be anything other than a Jesuit priest. Celibacy became a personal issue for me only when I gradually sensed that my choice of the single life long before had to be reviewed now. In the light of my much better informed understanding of celibacy and taking my fifteen years of celibate experience into account, I had to decide whether I could best serve the Lord as a single or as a married man.

There was never any question of whether I should be a priest. Up to this point, I had always accepted celibacy because it was a condition for being a priest. Service as a married priest had simply been an unthinkable form of life in my earlier years; the vocational literature had compared the married with the celibate state so unfavorably that priestly dedication seemed genuinely incompatible with the "lower" married state. But the terms of the issue were now redefined, and, in principle at least, I could be either single or married and still be a priest.

Which state did I really want to live in now, still choosing freely but with new light on the issues and their implications for the renewal of the Church? I realized, of course, that the Latin rite bishops opposed the restoration of a married clergy and that a decision to marry would involve me in a struggle whose end and outcome I could not foresee or control. But I had to make the choice, one way or another, as my conscience directed; to evade this decision would have meant my failure as a priest to take up the share of the Church's renewal pains that my graces best fitted me to bear. It was some comfort to realize that in the Church's long history her most faithful sons and daughters were normally not her most respected or welcome members.

The decision to marry was the most difficult judgment I had ever made. I had to convince myself that I was losing neither my faith nor my mind in asking the hitherto unthinkable questions. It was a common presumption only a short time ago that no priest left to marry without being either derelict or mentally ill. It was, and in official writings remains, inconceivable that a priest could decide to marry with a well-formed conscience. The pressure to dismiss the question "Is marriage part of my vocation?" as a temptation to be fled from was almost irresistible.

The effort to evaluate the substantive issues as well as my mental and emotional state took several months and much labor. I began with intensive study of all the literature I could find that explored the pros and cons of the status quo and of change to optional celibacy. I prayed often for light to see the truth, and I carefully examined the traditional counsels to priests, particularly those of the respected fellow Jesuit Karl Rahner.

As my analysis of the problem began to take shape, I exposed my thoughts to older priests and religious superiors, particularly to men whose skill as counselors was widely respected and who, I judged, knew and loved me well enough to help me see my most subtle self-deception. It was a lonely period of my life. I could not share my struggles with most of the men who shared my daily routine. Sometimes I wept a little when I thought of what it would be like to be a Jesuit priest no longer and to live in that undefined no-man's land of priests who marry.

The study, prayer, and consultation gradually clarified the decision I must make. Marriage was as much a part of my vocation as was priesthood. For my own sake as well as for the sake of others I had to try to win a place for married priests in the Church. My psychological and emotional makeup was not uniquely suited for marriage or for celibacy. I felt free to choose between these two states of life. My commitment to priesthood did not compel one choice or the other, either. I simply believed that it would be best for my own good and for the good of the Church if I asserted my desire to be a married priest. At the same time I could explain the many reasons why the Church ought to make room within her rules for this exercise of responsible Christian freedom.

My training (as an economist) fitted me, I thought, to help pioneer a self-supporting married clergy that, through its secular involvements, could reach groups not normally in touch with the parish staffs and even donate its services to the Church. My personal experience and study made me able to work for a restoration of optional celibacy without impugning the values of the freely chosen single life. And, above all I then thought, I could help Church authorities to see the objective case for change; since I had no emotional involvement or specific plans to marry, they would not dismiss my case as a mere rationalization.

The months that followed this decision and my initial efforts to gain an official hearing produced an unexpected and thoroughly shocking phase of my Catholic education. I discovered the refusal of the official Church to explore the issues I had raised. There was not the slightest effort to evaluate the conscience I had formed so carefully according to all the approved norms. The judgment of those in authority was clear: no conscience in conflict with a Church law could be a good conscience; or, as one man put it, the Holy Spirit does not give vocations that the Church does not recognize. A priori, I was denied any hearing for a discussion of the merits of my request. My most painful discovery, I have to admit, was that, for Church authorities, it was praiseworthy but irrelevant that I was emotionally uninvolved. In no way did this suggest to them that the case I presented had objective merit. Rather I suspect it conveyed the suspicion that I would not act on my convictions and, ultimately, would let the matter die.

It was hard to stay uninvolved during those long months of decision. But I could not offer to share my life with anyone until I had gained a surer sense of direction. Perhaps those who are unacquainted with the decision-making habits that a Jesuit learns must view my efforts to choose rightly as cold, abstract, and almost inhuman. The Jesuit approach to such life-shaking judgments begins with a mighty effort to free oneself from disordered affections and to focus on the fundamental values of a Christian life. It is an all-out attempt to muster the light and courage to choose freely the highest values one can perceive.

The technique that suited me is surely not an apt one for everyone else. But it did produce a decision I could happily live with. I worried at times that I might be fighting for a right I could never exercise. Who could guarantee that I would ever find the "right" partner for marriage, or that I could successfully make the adjustments from bachelor habits to the sensitivities required of a good husband? The fears were not idle ones, but the Ignatian wisdom that demanded uninvolvement at this stage was more compelling. If I was genuinely free to choose either marriage or the single life and I chose the highest value for me, it would be a choice on which I could rest my life and salvation.

It was a wonderful grace to find my way to a decision that could give me inner peace. But if one is allowed to rank God's gifts, it was a richer grace yet to find the person who is now my wife. To describe my discovery of her as a grace is no pious exaggeration. I was demanding extraordinary qualities of the woman I would marry and I had to perceive those qualities before I dated her. Both she and I believe that our lives would never have crossed if the Lord had not so arranged them.

I first began looking for a marriage partner when I realized that Church authorities were no more likely to listen to an uninvolved priest than to one who had already married. In fact, the contrary was the case: those who transgressed the law (of celibacy) were more quickly dispensed from it. And so I made the careful judgment that so long as I minimized the likelihood of scandal, there was no reason not to begin looking for a marriage partner.

Judging from my own experience, I suspect that few priests who marry would ever want to relive the process of getting engaged. It was an unnerving time for me because a single error of judgment would have had unusually painful personal consequences. Everyone who marries, of course, goes through the search for someone with whom there is mutual attraction. As a priest who wanted to stay a priest, however, I had to find someone who would also love me as a priest and who would share my interest in the ministry. With me she would have to bear with the disapproval of the Church and with its threats of punishment. And even if such a woman came into sight, I would still have to trust my instincts enough to tell her of my plans—and, as my wife has told me, she had to have the good sense not to act so coy that I would lose my nerve.

To our everlasting surprise, my wife—Pat—and I passed the initial hurdles and began to make our plans for marriage. We decided not to marry right away for several reasons: we needed time to get to know each other better, and we both believed that, given time, the Church would bless our marriage.

We certainly needed time to discover each other more fully and to enjoy each other's company. After all, we began to date only after we became engaged. Some months ago when we were being interviewed, I had to explain this unconventional approach and could only come up with a bit of painful humor: "After all, I couldn't ask her to dance *before* I asked her to marry me!"

However unconventional the beginning, those months brought us many wonderful hours—bittersweet sometimes, but wonderful nonetheless. I relearned, awkwardly at times, the beauty and the joy of a woman's love. And Pat learned of my strengths and weaknesses as her future husband. Thanks to our need for discretion, we normally stayed away from public places: dinner at her apartment, a movie at a neighborhood theater, a walk along quiet streets, this was the simple stuff of our time together, all made rich by our growing joy in being with each other.

Occasionally, we risked discovery and took in a Manhattan play or dinner at a midtown restaurant. I was always edgy about these excursions and took almost irrational precautions to minimize the chance of being seen by an acquaintance. We never went to good fish houses on a Friday evening, for instance; experience warned me that the clergy would be found there in force. The constant discretion we had to exercise was a very dark cloud in our lives. We were so careful about hiding our relationship from those who knew me as a priest that sometimes, when we were apart from each other, we both had the feeling that it was all a dream, wholly unrelated to the normal stuff of our daily lives. Pat often felt that if I died suddenly no one would ever know of her.

Slowly we discovered each other, and together we faced the high cost of my desire to be a married priest. Bit by bit we fit this cost into our growing budget of mutual love. We paid the first installment as we met the price of my continued commitments as a priest. My increasing love for Pat did not lead me to withdraw from priestly work; to the contrary, I seemed to get more deeply involved. We often discussed my ideas for sermons or for talks, and Pat helped me to strive for relevance in all I said. Often, she patiently bore my absence when my work as a priest kept us apart. Pat quietly taught me that I could love her and be a better priest. Far from dividing my heart, she made it more dedicated, more sensitive to the common human troubles to which the Gospel must speak.

My wife also helped me face a more upsetting side of my desire to be a married priest. If I had to choose between marriage and continued official good standing as a priest, I had to choose the former. I hated to face the apparent dilemma. We both believed firmly that the Church would listen and, ultimately, would approve our marriage. But I had to face the likelihood that the Church's response would be No. What then? Pat was deeply bothered by my unwillingness to face the question. It was reasonable to wonder whether she should really give her life to me if I was so unsure of my gift of love to her.

One night, while walking home from a movie, I finally saw the only answer I could live with. Faced with such a choice, I would marry. She was a gift the Lord had put into my hands, and graces can bear fruit only if one takes them when the Lord chooses to make us rich with them. Originally, I had my own plan of salvation for myself: first, the Church's acceptance of my conscience; then, the discovery of my wife-to-be; and, overall, the approval and admiration of others for our actions. I had to learn the Lord's unlikely path for me: the Church's silence in response to my reasoned and respectful request; the decision to sacrifice my right to function as a priest so that I would be worthy to lead others in celebrating the Lord's sacrifice; the choice of an uncertain, wildly unpredictable future as a married priest to replace the secure and well-planned career of the priest many wanted me to be.

In her love for me, I think my wife grasped this profound paradox long before I could put the same thing into words that satisfied my conscience. Very simply, I had to be willing to put off my Roman collar and to give up my priestly jobs—the external signs of priesthood—if I really wanted to be a faithful priest of God. Doing so, I gained a deeper knowledge of what Christian priesthood means. I had no right to consecrate if I balked at putting my own body on the line, when the Lord designated it as the gift to be transformed.

The months before our marriage were not only a time of discovering each other; they were also a time of trying to gain the Church's approval for our marriage. We realized that other couples shared our desires and we hoped that, joined together, we could convince the Church that it should respect our consciences and bless our Christian marriages. With several other priests, then, I helped to found the National Association for Pastoral Renewal, a nationwide organization open to priests and to laity that sought to open up an official discussion of the celibacy problem in the United States.

This essay is not the place to tell the story of NAPR's founding and early history. I only refer to it as a proof of the seriousness of our desire to change the Church's rules. With other founding members, I helped to write the NAPR position paper on celibacy, a statement that has had an immeasurable impact on discussion of the topic ever since. I was also the general coordinator of opinion surveys on celibacy that reached half of all United States diocesan priests, and prepared a final report on the survey results that reportedly found its way to Pope Paul's desk. Pat was active in these early efforts, stuffing and stamping and counting returns, and always encouraging me not to lose hope. It was an unusual occupation for a time of courtship, but it was a time of shared hope—and disappointment—that we'll never regret.

Gradually, the passing months dashed our hopes of being heard. After Pope Paul officially reaffirmed the law of celibacy, the father general of the Jesuits decided that he could not request an official hearing for my case and I had to leave the Society of Jesus. Although I had not incurred any Church punishment, I was now without a bishop and was abruptly barred from any priestly work. It was a hard change after five and a half years of ministry. However clearly you foresee such an event, its reality is always an unwelcome surprise.

This couldn't be happening to me, I thought. Many friends and relatives were a great support at this time. They wrote long letters and short notes to assure me of their love and understanding and, often, of their admiration. With few exceptions they respected my conscience and encouraged me to continue my struggle for the renewal of the Church. I only wish that Pope Paul and fellow bishops who fear that Catholics are scandalized by the prospect of a married clergy could read the letters I received. They might learn that men and women of great faith disagree profoundly with the official insistence that priests must live as celibates.

Pat and I now accepted the fact that the Church was not likely to approve me as a married priest. So we did our best to secure the Church's blessing for our marriage. We quickly learned that, once again, no one with authority would listen to our request. I was advised to direct my appeal to Archbishop Paul Philippe in the Vatican office that handles appeals for dispensation from celibacy. Successive letters went unanswered over a period of five months. The date for our marriage approached and the Church would not even acknowledge our letters. It was a terrible burden for our families. Like us, they found it incredible that Church officials would not even have the courtesy to answer letters; unlike us, they were reluctant to believe that a Catholic can marry, validly and without suffering excommunication, when the Church will not sanction the union.

We thought our problem through as carefully as we could. Both of us loved the Church and had no intention of cutting ourselves off from it. We believed as Catholics and wanted to profess our Catholic faith in our exchange of married love. It was repugnant to us to plan to marry in a somehow invalid, nonsacramental way—for instance, before a justice of the peace—even if this would quickly gain us Church approval for a Catholic wedding. And, in all honesty, we felt we could not go through with one of the secret chancery weddings that are sometimes permitted by Church authorities.

We did what we could, and we believe that so far as it was within our power, our wedding was a valid, sacramental, and very Catholic act. An Episcopal priest friend of ours helped us to work out a ceremony that respected the faith and traditions of both of our Churches. A Catholic priest and a Catholic woman served as the official witnesses of our exchange of vows. Nearly one hundred fellow Catholics joined us in celebrating the marriage, and in brief remarks to them at the end I told them of our love for the Church and our intention to express our Catholic faith.

Admittedly, no official representative of the Church came to our wedding, but the Church never bothered even to refuse our invitation and request. How could such a marriage condemn us, as Church officials claimed it would? In fact, Canon Law excuses Catholics from the requirement of marrying before a priest when no priest is available and the marriage would be delayed for an unreasonable period. Moreover, our earnest efforts to secure the Church's blessing certainly preserved us from the evil intent required for any excommunication. Then and now, we are at peace with the Church, and someday soon we hope for some sign that Church authorities are willing to be at peace with us.

This has been a brief account of how I became a married priest, married and still a priest. I still celebrate Mass whenever anyone believes enough in my priesthood and loves the Church enough to join together in celebrating the Lord who saves us. We still hope that I will soon be accepted again for public ministry in the Church. We hope that the Church will soon accept and bless our Christian marriage. We are ready to support any reasonable effort to achieve these goals and promote renewal in the Church we love and refuse to leave.

I have joined the Society of Priests for a Free Ministry and continue to serve on the board of directors of NAPR. If we find other ways to prove that we have not abandoned my call to priesthood, we will take these up, too. We see no reason why I should give up my will to serve as a priest.

The Church is now in the painful throes of renewal, and she desperately needs the dedication of those who love her. Pat and I do love the Church. We have discovered the seamy side of the institution in our effort to change the law of celibacy. But the evils the Church does in the name of Christ are a reason not for leaving her but for renewed dedication to her renewal. The Church desperately needs all the sons and daughters who really believe she can measure up to her own high ideals of what the Church of Christ must be. The Church needs her persistent, loving critics as well as patient, resilient victims of her unchristian acts. She needs priests and laity who profoundly believe that the Church becomes more full of life each time her members obey the Spirit who writes the law of love on all our hearts. Official approval or disapproval is a passing thing; the Spirit alone remains the rule of life. Fortified by these beliefs and joined to my loving wife, then, I have not and cannot leave the Church or the priesthood that I love.

13

I HEARD A VOICE

by George L. Weber

George L. Weber was born on April 10, 1929, in Bad Axe, Michigan. Upon graduating from Maryknoll Seminary in June 1950, he received the B.A. degree and upon completion of his theological studies at Maryknoll was ordained as a priest of the Catholic Foreign Mission Society of America, commonly known as Maryknoll Fathers. After ordination he attended the University of Notre Dame, where he secured his M.A. degree in English literature.

This was followed by two years of minor seminary teaching, one year in Mountain View, California, and the other in Clark Summit, Pennsylvania. In 1958, he was assigned to work in the diocese of Shinyanga, Tanzania, East Africa. For two years he did general missionary work, establishing outstations and teaching catechumens. During his last four years in Africa he was involved in building and directing a leadership training school, designed to prepare young lay couples to become a task force of salaried catechists.

While directing the school Father Weber helped develop agricultural programs in the surrounding villages and set up the first rural credit union in free Tanzania. In 1965 he was appointed rector of the major seminary at Maryknoll, New York, and continued in this capacity until his departure from the active ministry in January 1968.

I had just walked out of my post as rector of Maryknoll Seminary a few hours before and was wandering among the skyscrapers of New York City. I had written up my request for laicization and included a petition for dispensation from the obligation of clerical celibacy. These were in my former superior's possession and would soon be forwarded to Rome with his own letter of recommendation.

As I walked through the throngs of people, I was a bit self-conscious about wearing a tie; I was not quite used to being totally ignored, or should I say totally accepted as one of themselves, by the mass of lay people brushing by me. For the first time in my adult life I was "on my own," totally responsible for my future livelihood, sink or swim.

"Do you want to be a priest?" My answer had to be Yes to this question from a priest-psychologist friend just a few days before. "You're a good priest, George, a good priest," was his quiet response. I knew he meant it and I knew what he said was basically true, but every ounce of honesty within me knew that from one point of view I could never agree with him. I was in love; many times over I guess, but totally committed to one beautiful, deep, contemplative soul from the only point of view that I wanted to live.

It was not something I had planned; nor just something that had happened. Three and a half years previously I had returned from six years of missionary work in Tanzania, East Africa. It had been the greatest six years a man could ask for, from a traditional frame of reference. Born on a farm, I adapted readily to an agricultural people. The language came easily and the work was appealing. I had set up outstations, directed a leadership training school, and helped establish the first rural credit union in free Tanzania.

My society had assigned me to positions of responsibility: consultor to the regional superior in Africa and rector of the major seminary in New York. Retreat work, conferences, guest lectures, homilies, appealed to the deepest resources of my faith. In Africa I had struggled to convert the principles of Pope John XXIII's encyclicals *Mater et Magistra* and *Pacem in Terris* into viable social programs suited to local conditions. As rector I strove to be more pastor than administrator in my relationship with the seminarians.

As a student of the "new theology" I was searching painfully but optimistically for ever richer insights into my own identity and function as a priest within the community of the People of God. My life and my work placed me in daily contact with some of the most poetic, dedicated, practical men and women on the face of the earth. I rejoiced in their friendship and strove manfully to be daily more worthy of it.

But with each passing year after ordination this became more and more impossible. A priest's heart, by the Church's definition and desire, must be celibate and mine was no exception. The time came when truth to myself and truth to the Church and the priesthood I love demanded that I petition for release from the obligation of celibacy even at the grave cost of forfeiting my right to remain in the active ministry.

Many contacts with women in every walk of life contributed to this ultimate decision. Since the seventh grade I had been writing to Sisters whose prayers and interest supported me through thirteen years of seminary training and twelve years in the priesthood. They knew, no doubt far better than I, that the ability to live a life of love for everybody without being "in love" with anybody is not the gift of a moment on ordination day. It must be cultivated from early manhood with discipline and determination and reinforced each day with dedication and prayer. Most of all one must see it as a gift and not as a burden.

The motivation to live it must derive from the spirit of Christ's own celibate heart and thrive on an intimate communion with that heart through daily spiritual reading and meditation. How often I heard in the seminary that carelessness about praying the office each day was one of the first signs of impending disaster. The "disaster," of course, was defection from the priesthood, usually followed by marriage. The official stance of the Church toward such men always struck me as awesomely severe.

Privately I learned, as I grew older, that bishops and priests alike performed many quiet kindnesses whenever possible for their departed fellow priests. Almost always the kindness included offers to finance the removal of the "fallen priest" from the area lest his presence be a scandal to the faithful. Inwardly I quailed at the thought of meeting men who had given up their priesthood. I never dreamed I would one day join their ranks. In the seminary I was embarrassed if I heard a priest swear or saw a priest using liquor imprudently.

I never dated a girl, and throughout my seminary career never drank or smoked. My outlets came through sports and study; my motivation found its roots in silent prayer. My Thomistic background had neatly categorized values and virtues; seminary training scheduled daily living into predictable patterns designed to fill each moment with maximal meaning. Though never a scholar, I respected scholarship and enjoyed intellectual challenges.

My friendships were few, but they were deep and rich, poetic and comfortably masculine. Apart from a few Sisters with whom I corresponded infrequently, the women in my life were always "family." If someone had asked me what I thought about celibacy, I could have honestly answered that I didn't think of it at all. The topic had not yet hit the popular press. Catholic psychologists were still a few years away from canonizing it as a legitimate "in word" in clerical circles.

When I came back from Africa in the summer of 1964 after six years abroad, I was convinced from personal experience that new approaches were needed. It was gratifying to find that trained psychologists in my own society had recognized and researched the question and were beginning to publish their conclusions. They were not creative, nor were they expected to be. They were mostly descriptive and diagnostic. Sex in seminary training could no longer be handled with silence and separation.

This was the era of Salinger, Buber, and Teilhard de Chardin. Merleau-Ponty and Kwant stressed that we don't simply exist, we coexist. Rogers and Turner proved dialogue at deeply personal levels essential to growth in self-identity. Gibran, Saint-Exupéry, and Cummings voiced the same theme in poetry and song. I personally thrilled at the liberating forces contained in much of this and other similar material. The "open window" spirit of Pope John XXIII and the updating theme of Vatican II were richly detailed by Rahner, Schillebeecks, and a host of contemporary theologians.

We were breaking down barriers through ecumenical exposure and setting up senates at diocesan levels.

My faith was restored in the power of the Spirit at work within the Church. I accepted the major seminary rectorship all alive with desires to be daily more worthy of the men I served. I was determined to listen at every level and be credible to men as a man who shared their triumphs and felt their failures. I wanted to be involved in what was happening in human hearts, not so much as an administrator who must judge worthiness, but more as a fellow missioner who encouraged men to trust their hearts and use their heads. I wanted theologians to emerge from our program who could identify with the mission of the Church, preach it intelligently, and support it with a passion for prayer.

While in Africa I was confronted for the first time in my life with the constant physical presence of women. Nakedness in our culture was either sold for cheap profit at the gutter level or shrouded in secret and silence within the privacy of marriage. Nakedness in Africa was neither flaunted nor feared. More of it was acceptable, so one developed a greater emotional tolerance for it, externally at least. Internally I was fighting painful battles. I never really got used to having attractive women around. It was always a surprise, like that fantastic event called sunrise. Emotional involvements were out of the question. Friendships with women could never be explored since motives would rightly be suspect. I learned much about their emotions, but almost nothing about the persons who expressed them. We complained about the lack of love in marriage among our Christians and I knew I was struggling with the same issue in my own life.

During my last year in Africa I was treated for malaria, bilharzia, hookworm, and hepatitis. It took me almost a year to regain my strength after returning to the States. While resting I read a lot, shared a lot with priest friends, and fell in love for the first time in my life; not just once, but several times over. Suddenly my whole experience of Christian sign and symbol came alive at the level of feeling. I had finally met persons in my adult life who were women and to whom I could respond as a man who truly rejoiced in their unique beauty while respecting their vows. I know, under God, that they felt the same. They had to find Christ in someone, I had to share Him with someone.

Eventually I came to know who that someone had to be, and the day I did, I knew for me it had to be in marriage. I had not lost my respect for vows of virginity and celibacy, I merely knew suddenly and certainly that it was psychologically absurd to love someone the way I loved Julie and relinquish responsibility for her well being. We had no need or intention of changing our dedication to the truths we held dear.

On the contrary, we would be freed, in some ways, to pursue them more intensely. I knew from bitter experience that without the focal point of Julie's love alone, conflicts and crises would continue to arise in my relationships with women. I would end up spending so much energy keeping my psychic canoe from tipping over that I would have little left to row it against the tide of life. I sat down and wrote:

> Your word, Lord, comes silently today.
> Tomorrow it may shout.
> But always without forcing
> It draws us to decision.
>
> In season the leaf must fall,
> > the bud must break
> > the flower bloom—
> All in its season, and you and I
> Must wait upon that season.
>
> But when it comes, it comes
> Just once for every leaf and bud and flower.
> > No other hour is so precious
> > So full of providence
> > So full of word.
> Then tears fall into love
> > And smile!

The late Senator Robert Kennedy was asked during his brother's administration why he had accepted the position of Attorney General after stating categorically during the Wisconsin primary campaign that he would not consider taking such an appointment, should his brother be elected. The senator's succinct reply? "I changed my mind!" There is something beautifully direct and disarming about that answer, even something satisfying. It brought down the house at the banquet where he made the statement.

I have envied the directness and finality of that answer more than once over the past few months. But for me it just couldn't work. Too much was involved in stepping out of the priesthood and the responsibilities of celibacy. To say simply that I had changed my mind would sound ludicrous to some and sacrilegious to others. I have always believed my old novice master's remark: "To kid someone else is a venial sin, but to kid yourself is a mortal sin."

I am as susceptible to pride and human respect as the next man. It was not pleasant to anticipate what others might say of my decision. I was not a child when I accepted freely the responsibility of celibacy. Since we are taught in theology that sufficient grace, or help from God, is given to each priest to enable him to carry out his commitment, obviously I had failed to cooperate with this grace. What was it? Wine, women, or song? Punch or Judy?

In my twelve years in the priesthood I had cringed more than once at the ribald humor and shallow self-satisfaction of just a few men who mixed such questions in with their drinks, ignorant no doubt of their own insensitivity, as they matched bromide against bromide until supper was served. I could rightly expect to become the object of such humor. It would hurt, not because it was so outlandish and so false, but because it was so uncritical and half true. Never could I appreciate more sharply G. K. Chesterton's comment about the most dangerous kinds of truths being half-truths.

An imposing bank of bishops in a crowded courtroom pronounced Joan of Arc a fraud for failing to produce visions, which she claimed to enjoy frequently in the privacy of her prayers. One who actually believed in Joan would have accepted the visions as the celebration or overflow of her intense state of contemplation. Those who laughed her to scorn and eventually supported her death sentence interpreted her visions and her voices as subtle self-delusions and her insistence on following them as dangerous exhibitionism. There was a half-truth in the bishops' doubts, and a half-truth in the common man's faith in Joan.

Only Joan knew the whole truth, which proved brighter than the right reason of the bishops and broader than the full faith of the throng. The greatest violence done to Joan was done by herself. She was violently opposed to avoiding the voices by avoiding her prayers, and equally opposed to denying the voices which visited her in prayer. She would simply be Joan.

She would live with her God as her conscience commanded and believe in the face of fire that Holy Mother Church asked no more nor less from any of her children. It was at the knees of this same Mother that she had learned to pray, not in search of voices but in response to the Spirit. The Church can define all the types of prayer, but she can never presume to know how the Spirit will respond to them in individual situations.

The same must be said today. I never dreamed of praying for a love that would lead to marriage, but it was through prayer that that love truly blossomed. I never prayed for the courage to leave the priesthood, but I know that prayer brought that courage when the time for decision arrived. Wiser men than I have hinted that I just didn't catch myself soon enough. They suggested that psychological help a few years ago could have "saved my vocation." Once a man says Yes to an "illicit love," it is virtually impossible to talk sense to him. I have no defense. I only know that if crooked lines have brought me to where I am, then, for the first time in my life, I can repeat Claudel's comment of some years ago that God draws straight with crooked lines and does so with the full freedom of faith.

A few weeks after leaving my post as major seminary rector, I read part of the annual report from the Bishops Conference in Washington, D.C. It referred to those who left the priestly ministry as "derelicts." I had already met several inactive priests who had married and were fairly well settled in their new responsibilities as husbands, fathers, and breadwinners. Not by the farthest stretch of the imagination could I see them as derelicts. Something way down inside of me kept saying that this was all one great big mistake.

A line from Hopkins popped into my head more than once at these times: "Oh, if they knew what they do when they cut and hew, hack and rack the growing green." It was obvious that the bishops were blinded by an appalling ignorance of the hearts and heads of hundreds of men who loved the Church dearly, and for that very reason knew they must leave the active ministry in favor of marriage.

Many of them, myself included, would return to the ministry tomorrow if they could be free from parochial structures and permitted to function as worker-priests, lost like leaven in the dough, dying to the rubrics of tipped hats on subways, discounts at stores, and tax-free salaries, and alive to the awful poverty of each day's call to responsible work for a reasonable income. God knows I point no fingers of derision at my fellow priests in the active ministry. Too many of them are still cherished friends of mine. Too many of them could articulate more artfully than I the many burning hopes we share in common. It is not a question of "either/or" when it comes to a married or celibate, a salaried or unsalaried ministry. There is more than room for both. There is no reason why they wouldn't complement one another in many healthy ways.

I personally see no other alternative. More hetero-social relationships are not just permitted in modern seminaries, they are being strongly recommended by leading psychologists, priests as well as laymen. Healthy hearts are hetero-socially oriented hearts and the Church wants her ministers healthy. Various suggestions have been made by sincerely creative minds. We are encouraged to open seminary training programs to female faculty members and allow seminarians access to co-ed campuses whenever possible.

Seminarians and young Sisters work together in catechetical programs and inner-city poverty programs. At a time in life when most unmarried men and women are meeting regularly and happily to choose the most perfect mate, our seminarians and young Sisters are meeting regularly and hopefully to prepare the most perfect syllabus. We can call it hetero-social orientation programs or health clinics for celibate students. We can even refrain from calling it anything and accept it as a step toward normalcy in our training programs.

My personal opinion is that many priest psychologists promoting hetero-social contacts are already convinced, consciously or unconsciously, that celibacy should be in fact optional, and that their creative programs are doing everything that is psychologically wholesome to promote the issue. I am not saying that they do not believe in celibacy, but that they do not believe in compulsory celibacy as a requisite for effective priestly ministry. Some, whom I know personally, are deeply in love with beautifully dedicated Christian women whom they have met, usually by chance, in the course of their ministry. I admire endlessly their ability to maintain frequent if not daily contact with these women through phone calls and letters without letting it distract from their celibate commitment to the whole People of God.

Actually it is the women in such relationships who suffer much more than the men. Often they are Sisters whose love for a man can only be justified as their love for Christ made incarnate or as a unique gift of mystical marriage. This is one case where mysticism, to my mind, is probably half mist and half schism. But there must undoubtedly be exceptions to prove this rule. One priest psychologist used the analogy of a wheel. One woman's love is a "hub" relationship around which all others revolve like spokes. But how much suspicion, jealousy, and heartbreak can result when these human spokes have hopes of becoming the "hub," or worse yet, actually think they are!

Shortly after leaving the seminary for good, I spoke in this vein for almost an hour with a priest of my age who had a degree in clinical counseling. He was an elected diocesan senator and highly sensitive to his responsibilities to the younger men whom he represented. When I had finished my story describing my reasons for leaving, he surprised me by rising suddenly, walking over to where I was seated, and shaking my hand. "It is truly a grace to meet such a thoroughly honest man, George!" he remarked. "God has given you a great gift!"

He then sat down and told me his own story. He was in love to the tips of his fingers with a woman who shared his love for the priesthood. He knew her anguish as their hopes waned for a quick change in the Church's policy on celibacy. He knew the younger priests counted on his influence and felt it would take at least two years to accomplish what was necessary to justify their faith in him. He was just praying for the grace to hold off marriage for that length of time, and he was grateful that I shared his conviction that a priest committed to celibacy and a woman with the vow of virginity cannot support a deep emotional involvement indefinitely without opting for marriage or agreeing to drift apart. It appears to be just that simple. And, unfortunately, those who choose marriage must do so at the price of their active priesthood.

In examining my own reasons for leaving, I know that the major issue was celibacy, but it was not the only issue. It has been said that to succeed in life a man must work hard, think big, and have a dream. Something intuitive within me, something as deep as my faith in God and Christ and Mary's role in redemption, told me that the time had come to put my very life on the line as a witness to the fact that change must come in Church law and Church structure, and that it can come without fear that, in men like myself, faith will falter and fail.

I know bishops who believe privately that a married clergy will come in this century and that the official position on birth control will change with the next Pope. Without compromising the indissolubility of marriage, I feel divorce in certain circumstances is a Christian solution to a patent mistake on the part of two people. I have seen non-

Christian marriages broken "in favor of the faith" of one or both parties who wish to become Christians so that they can marry someone they truly love. If the Church is so merciful to the unbaptized, can she be less merciful to those who from earliest years have called her Mother?

I don't speak of condoning weakness. I speak of respecting the very core of a person's conscience. A young mother abandoned in her late teens by a drunken husband, who is known to have remarried and moved, should have the freedom to determine in her own heart whether remarriage is a fruitful decision for herself and her children, especially when the alternative is almost always prostitution in one form or another in some African cultures.

My own bishop in Africa wrote just this past year that the Church would do well to reconsider the demands it makes on husbands of polygamous marriages who seek baptism. I agree totally with the bishop. In particular instances it seems cruel and basically unchristian to force a man who seeks baptism to withdraw support and shelter from elderly women who have given him children and faithful service over many years in accord with local custom. Extreme hardship is placed on these women for the remainder of their lives.

If they return to their husband out of sheer need, he is refused the sacraments for as long as he keeps them in the shelter of his household. If they have been baptized in the meantime, they, too, are cut off from the Church's sacramental life. I find this solution more harsh than the heart of Christ reflected in the Gospels. Bishops should be empowered to make exceptions in such cases in the name of true Christian charity. The Church would not relinquish laws of sacramental moment. She would rather extend the full moment of Christian consent to baptism and marriage beyond the uttered word alone and let it include respect for past personal commitments, made in good faith, and continued responsibilities which flow from these commitments toward innocent parties whose own faith might well be strengthened and supported thereby.

Too often the law would have everything black and white; yet, many a mission bishop, I am sure, has felt that his Christians were 50-percent pagan and his pagans 50-percent Christian. Must the very sacraments required to strengthen a community in fraternal charity be refused, in the name of law, to those who in laudable good faith live up to their commitments to provide for and protect their wives of many years?

For me confessional work in the States became more and more psychologically impossible when dealing with young married couples. I could not in conscience uphold traditional positions on birth control. I became gradually convinced that I had best live my personal views on a more private level than was possible in the confessional.

"But," someone may ask, "didn't falling in love color your whole outlook toward sex and its various modes of expression? Wasn't this the real reason behind your hesitancy to function as a confessor? If you had kept a grip on your heart, would you not have put more trust in the teaching magisterium of the Church?" True, but it misses the point.

When a man says that he sees blue whenever he is angry, I cannot disqualify the veracity of his remark on the grounds that he was emotionally disturbed when his vision was colored. Yes, I was definitely emotionally involved. For me being in love was an essential ingredient in the total experience of "seeing" colors beyond the present narrow spectrum of possibility painted by conservative theologians. I did not seek out this experience. I even resisted it for years out of respect for vows and desire for "higher Virtue."

But now I can gratefully rejoice in the full responsibility of my love for Julie. Our relationship brings substance and celebration to our daily search for God at levels beyond laws. I was aware that I would finally embrace this life-giving commitment to Julie at the cost of pain to others. At the moment of truth I knew this pain could purify the hearts of all concerned because its source was honesty reaching to the very center of my soul.

All was the same, yet nothing was the same. Old thoughts had new meaning in this world of change and progress. It was I who had changed. I who had sung before of sun and rain and swaying trees, of time and silence, could now repeat the song—and yet it was a different song because the singer was new today.

I had thought about existence, and the more I sought it in mental flights, the more it had passed me by. It is a gift to trust one's intuitions. I had come to do that and to know therein is found the voice of God. I had come to a personal awareness at the center of my being and knew then that the Kingdom of God was within me. I had known another's love of the purest, human kind, all filled with faith and free from pride; and peace had put a new fire at work within me. The melody in my heart was singing:

Somewhere between the lines
Beyond the thought, outside of time
You dwell where eyes meet eyes
And fingers touch and hearts take heart.
You own that part of me that's locked
To any other key but your soft yes,
The fullness of your breast embracing mine.

It means in say, it says in speech
But is, and be, is out of reach
Of word. To feel, to sigh, to satisfy
The silence with assent to silent prayer.
Yes! Here creation cups its hands and overflows
With all the vastness of your singing soul
And plunges mine into the melody.

I came to feel at home in the world of space and time, and its groans
I heard and understood anew. I embraced hope with new desire to see
birth give way to growth and then to feel the smile of wisdom which
breathes respect for freedom.

There is a voice mocking violence today and stirring men to simply
be who they simply are. I had heard this voice as the memory of a
time when mercy plunged into my heart, and God forgave, and God
forgot. The voice was there that day and lingers on. I had heard it in
the written words of men of hope who cherish all creation and trust its
evolutionary trends, nor fear its shallow sins. I had heard this voice
as an echo of the glance of first love. I had heard it as the answer to
an ever-growing friendship.

This voice is abroad in the world today.

14

MARRIAGE:
AN INALIENABLE RIGHT

by John A. O'Brien

Does the priestly ministry require by its nature the state of celibacy? Should irrevocable, lifelong celibacy be demanded of a man as an indispensable requisite for ordination? May not a man have a vocation to the priesthood and not to celibacy? If so, why should we not have in Latin rite both a celibate and a married priesthood as in the Eastern rite churches? These are questions being widely discussed in rectories, monasteries, seminaries, living rooms, offices, newspapers, magazines, on radio and television. To find the answers let us turn first to the Bible.

In the Old Testament marriage and procreation are highly extolled, whereas the single state is greatly depreciated. The first chapter of Genesis relates: "God created man to his own image: to the image of God he created him: male and female he created them. And God blessed them, saying: 'Increase and multiply, and fill the earth, and subdue it'" (27–28).

The second chapter further unfolds the divine plan: "Wherefore a man shall leave father and mother, and shall cleave to his wife: and they shall be two in one flesh" (24). From these texts it is clear not only that marriage is a good and blessed thing, but also that it is normal for man and that he has an inalienable right to it. Thus does the first book of the Bible depict God's design for the marriage, love, and happiness of His children as well as the intimate interdependence and intercommunion of man and woman, each of whom finds his complement and fulfillment in the other.

In the New Testament both Christ and St. Paul modify the somewhat one-sided glorification of the married state by declaring that the single life is also a legitimate way of seeking the Kingdom of God. Our Lord indicates that "there are eunuchs who have made themselves such for the kingdom of heaven's sake" (Matt. 19:12). The interpretation of these words is not easy, but it is clear that the number of such eunuchs is small and embraces only those who are specifically called.

In the first Epistle to the Corinthians St. Paul says that "each one has his own gift from God, one in this way, and another in that" (7:6). Making clear that he has no command from God, he voices merely his own opinion in commanding the unmarried, free from the concerns of the world and able to think "about the things of God." Neither the words of Christ nor those of St. Paul are directed specifically or exclusively to priests or candidates for holy orders but to Christians generally. They simply indicate that the state of being unmarried for the sake of the kingdom of heaven can be an authentic way of Christian life.

In his first letter to Timothy, the Apostle Paul writes: "A bishop then, must be blameless, married but once, reserved, prudent, of good conduct, hospitable . . . He should rule well his own household, keeping his children under control and perfectly respectful . . . Deacons should be men who have been married but once, ruling well their children and their own households" (3:2, 4, 12).

That the Apostles were married is evident from the testimony of Paul himself. Writing to the Corinthians, he says: "Do we not have the right to be accompanied by a wife, as the other apostles of the Lord and Cephas?" (I Cor. 9:5). While *gune*, the word used here, can mean both woman and wife, the context, especially with the reference to Cephas (Peter), indicates that wife is here the most likely meaning.

While Paul is commonly thought of as a bachelor, not a few scriptural scholars think he was more probably a widower. Why? Because Paul boasted of himself as a devout and ardent follower of the Judaic Law and traditions, "a Hebrew of Hebrews; as regards the Law, a Pharisee"

(Philem. 3:5). Since Judaism took such a dim view of bachelors and held marriage in the highest esteem, they think Paul may have married early in life and was a widower at the time of writing his letters.

There is no line in the entire Bible which gives the slightest indication as to the state of life which the ecclesiastical minister should choose. He may be summoned to the state of virginity, but such a call is not directly connected with his vocation to the ministry. In the absence of any express prohibition, the minister can be expected to follow the law written deep in his very nature by the Creator and proclaimed at the dawn of creation: "Wherefore a man shall leave father and mother, and shall cleave to his wife: and they shall be two in one flesh."

This is precisely what the overwhelming majority of deacons, priests, presbyters, and bishops did in the early centuries, the golden era of the Christian faith. Hence all biblical scholars, theologians, and canonists are as one in emphasizing that the requirement of celibacy in the Latin rite Church is a purely ecclesiastical law that must stand or fall on its own merits.

In the Eastern rite church during the early centuries both bishops and priests, as in the apostolic era, were generally married. During the fourth century, due to neoplatonic ideas and Latin rite influences, the episcopacy became generally reserved for unmarried priests. If a married man was without children, he might be consecrated, provided he separated from his wife.

For all other clerics, however, the Trullan Synod (692) permitted marriage before ordination and the use of marriage rights afterward. By indirection, the synod criticized Latin marriage legislation by decreeing that if anyone should attempt to deprive a married priest, deacon, or subdeacon of his marriage rights, or if one of the aforesaid should renounce his wife "on the pretense of piety," he was to be condemned and deposed.

Let us look briefly at the history of celibacy in the Western Church. During the first three or four centuries deacons, priests, and bishops were free to marry and commonly did so. Commenting on the Pauline texts, Clement of Alexandria (c. 150–215) pointed out that marriage, properly used, is a way of salvation for all: priests, deacons, and laymen. In 345 the Synod of Gangra condemned manifestations of spurious asceticism, such as the refusal to attend divine worship celebrated by married clergy.

In 325, when the Council of Nicaea was held, the majority of priests and many bishops were married. The attempt of Bishop Hosius of Córdoba to have the council prohibit clerical marriage brought a vigorous protest from the Egyptian Bishop Paphnutius. Though himself unmarried, he declared that such a rule would be difficult and imprudent, and that celibacy should remain a matter of vocation and personal choice. The council followed his wise advice.

In the early centuries it was a not uncommon custom for a son to succeed his father as pastor or as bishop. Thus St. Gregory of Nazianzus succeeded his father as bishop and in Auvergne, France, Appolonaris followed his father as bishop. At Limoges, Ruricius II succeeded his grandfather, while the succession of Gregory the Illuminator, the first bishop of Armenia, remained in his family for four generations, passing from father to son.

As Christianity entered increasingly into the Greco-Roman world, its members came under the influence of Hellenic stoicism and widespread gnostic dualism. The latter erected a strong division between body and soul and relegated the body and all its activities to an inferior position. These tendencies to world-denial and rigorism led many Christians to depreciate marriage and transform St. Paul's counsel to chastity into a requirement for celibacy. Many Christian writers, notably Tertullian, Jerome, and Augustine, spoke disparagingly of wedlock, woman, and the conjugal act itself.

At a synod in Rome in 386, Pope Siricius sent a letter to Bishop Himerius of Tarragona in Spain, in which he termed the marriage act of clergy a crime and their desire for it "obscene cupidity." Characterizing the priests themselves as lustful people, he condemned their way of living with an appeal to such texts as Romans 8:8, I Peter 1:16, and Ephesians 5:27, which are totally irrelevant here. In similar vein St. Ambrose of Milan (339–97) warned that "the ministerial office must be kept pure and unspotted, and must not be defiled by coitus" and that the married priest is "foul in heart and body."

BALEFUL INFLUENCE OF AUGUSTINE

Of far greater influence upon Christian thinking concerning marriage and particularly the conjugal relation was St. Ambrose's famous disciple, St. Augustine (354–430). The son of a Christian mother and a pagan father, Augustine became infected, at the age of eighteen, with Manichaeism, the heresy which taught that matter and flesh are inherently evil, and that man achieves a release of the spirit by practicing rigorous asceticism, especially by obtaining from procreation and animal food.

From eighteen to twenty-nine, Augustine lived with a girl outside of wedlock. Of this union was born one child, conceived during the first year of their relationship. From this prolonged sexual liaison, in which unselfish love seems to have had little part, Augustine apparently drew many, if not most, of the concepts and ideas which dominated his writings on sex and marriage.

"Having had," points out Dr. John T. Noonan, "this guilt-ridden experience of sexual intercourse in a quasi-permanent union, Augustine believed there was nothing rational, spiritual, sacramental in the act of intercourse itself." In marriage, he finds but three goods: offspring, fidelity, and symbolic stability (*proles, fides, sacramentum*). Reflecting the remorse piled up through the years of his illegitimate union, he considers sexual intercourse in marriage as the greatest threat to spiritual freedom: "I feel that nothing more turns the masculine mind from the heights than female blandishment and that contact of bodies without which a wife may not be had."

One searches in vain for any mention of that holy love which the Almighty says will prompt man to leave father and mother and cleave to his wife until the two become "one flesh." One looks in vain for any hint of that sacred affection of wife and husband, which mirrors the love of Christ for the Church, of which Paul speaks so reverently: "Even thus ought husbands also to love their wives as their own bodies" (Eph. 5:28).

The chief thrust of Augustine's writings appears in his exegesis of the text in Genesis where the Almighty declares, "it is not good for man to be alone." Why? Augustine answers: "I do not see what other help woman would be to man if the purpose of generating would be eliminated." Augustine appears blind to one of the chief—if not the chief—joys of marriage: shared companionship.

SHAPED CATHOLIC THOUGHT

Even the pleasure of the conjugal act is looked upon at least as a regrettable concession to man's lust, if it is not positively sinful. Indeed, in a sermon he characterizes intercourse without procreative intent as a kind of sin which may, however, be cleansed by ordinary acts of

Christian charity, such as almsgiving. So ignoble and degrading was the act of coitus that Augustine normally required both the objective possibility of procreation and the subjective intent to procreate to give some justification for it.

For more than fifteen centuries—from the year 400 to recent times—Augustine's disparaging views profoundly influenced, when they did not completely dominate, Catholic theological thought. Embedded deep in his mind from his formative years were the Manichaean concepts of the inherent evil of matter and the flesh and the guilt-stained memories of his shameful liaison with the nameless young woman, so faithful and devoted to him through the years, but to whom he never had the decency to give his name in marriage. For the most part theologians have taken over his line of reasoning, without making allowance for the background that colored so much of his thinking.

Saturated with Augustine's thought, Thomas Aquinas adopts his views on the animal character of marital intercourse. "Beasts," he writes, "are without reason. In this way man becomes, as it were, like them in coition, because he cannot moderate the delight of intercourse and the heat of concupiscence by reason." Hence it is Augustine, the former profligate, who must bear, as the Dutch theologian R. J. Bunnik points out, "no small measure of responsibility for the insinuation into our culture of the idea, still widely current, that Christianity regards sexuality as something particularly tainted with evil."

With marriage regarded as a concession to human frailty and lust, and virginity a form of asceticism and heroism, it is easy to see how the ideal of permanent chastity or celibacy came to be applied to ecclesiastical ministers. This was accomplished, in part, by selecting an increasing number of ministers from the monasteries, where the ideal of lifelong chastity or virginity was held in such high esteem.

FORTY MARRIED POPES

Repeated efforts were made by synods, councils, and popes to impose celibacy first upon bishops and then upon lower clergy in the Church of the West. As they were struggling against one of the strongest drives of human nature, however, they met with but partial and intermittent success. Historians estimate that of the 262 popes approximately 40 were married legally and validly. In the fifth century the son of a priest was elected Pope: Felix II (483–92). This happened again in the sixth century: Agapetus (535–36). Even as late as the ninth century a married man ascended the papal throne: Adrian II (867–72).

In 1139 the second Lateran Council decreed that henceforth it would not be possible for an ecclesiastical minister in major orders to contract a valid marriage. While this decree marked the culmination of a long development in the legislation of the Latin Church, the actual situation underwent no marked change. Clerical marriage and concubinage were so deeply rooted in widespread custom that attempts to enforce the official legislation failed miserably. "Three centuries after Lateran II," reports R. J. Bunnik, "the situation had not considerably improved, and at the Council of Constance (1414–18) it was proposed to abrogate the law."

The end of the Middle Ages witnessed another period of decline in clerical morality. It was occasioned by the Hundred Years' War, the Black Death, the Western Schism, and especially the pagan spirit of the Renaissance, which penetrated even into the papacy. Clerical marriage was widespread; sons of priests were readily legitimized and, as in the case of Erasmus, even raised to the priesthood with a dispensation from the Roman Curia for a small offering.

The Emperor Ferdinand I and several princes recommended to Pius IV that Germany be granted a married priesthood as well as Communion under both species. Duke Albert V of Bavaria advised that only married men be ordained and that the Church be indulgent with priests who married. Despite the reform measures launched by the Council of Trent, there were still many who ignored the law of celibacy.

During the first years of the French Revolution many priests married. Napoleon's negotiations with Pius VII brought about the legalization of the marriages of the seculars. In the nineteenth century the secession of the Old Catholics led to the abrogation of the celibacy law in this Church. In 1920 the Slovak Catholic Union urged Rome to restore a married clergy for Bohemia.

Dr. Petro Bilaniuk of Toronto University, a prominent member of the Ukrainian Catholic Church in Canada, has publicly declared: "We believe that the introduction of a married clergy is long overdue in the Latin rite. The forceful introduction of celibacy, in 1929, into the life of the Ukrainian Catholic Church in Canada and the United States caused over 100,000 faithful to leave the Church and join the Ukrainian

Orthodox Church and some other Christian communities, as a protest against this imposition of a foreign Church discipline. We believe that the introduction of a married clergy into the discipline and life of the Latin Church will be an important move, and will bring great benefits to all Christianity."

TIME FOR A NEW DEAL

In most of the countries of the West an ever-increasing number of priests are asking for a reconsideration of the grounds for making celibacy an indispensable requisite for ordination. This is purely ecclesiastical legislation, they point out, for which there isn't a shred of evidence in either the Old or the New Testament.

In the fall of 1966, 1,700 of Holland's 5,000 diocesan priests signed a petition requesting the Dutch hierarchy to consider ending compulsory celibacy. The bishops have shown great sympathy with the problems of the 200 priests who have resigned from office in the past three years, many of them to marry. With Vatican permission, *Time* (3-31-67) reports, a few of the married clergy have been permitted to remain in their pastoral posts. In March 1966 the hierarchy established a "halfway house" to counsel priests who decided to seek laicization.

What makes urgently imperative the examination of the reasons for tying celibacy to the priesthood is the ever-increasing worldwide shortage of priests. Millions of nominal Catholics are dying each year without the sacraments because there are no priests to administer them. In Latin America alone the Church faces the loss of more than a hundred million souls in the next few decades because of the lack of priests. At the heart of that scarcity, it is generally agreed, is the requirement of lifelong celibacy.

Isn't this a pretty stiff price to pay for celibacy? Is this ecclesiastical law to take precedence over the command of Christ to "preach the Gospel to every creature," to "teach all nations," baptize, pardon, anoint, and feed them with the Bread of Angels?

"Is the requirement of celibacy," we asked the rector of a seminary, "a chief or major cause of seminarians dropping out?"

"Unquestionably," he replied. "Out of 100 students starting in the minor seminary, about 90 drop out before major orders. The maturing of the sex faculty during the intervening years opens their eyes to the fierce lifelong struggle they are facing.

"They decide they have no vocation. But what they really discover is that they have none for celibacy. Drop that requirement and the picture will quickly change."

"Unrealistic and Dehumanizing"

Strong corroboration of this fact is offered by Father Paul C. Diebels, Executive Director, Latin American Mission Program, Mexicali, Mexico. Writing in the *National Catholic Reporter*, he says: "After seven years in Latin America, four in Peru, and three in Mexico, I feel that one of the strong contributory factors to the low regard in which the local people hold the native clergy is the unrealistic and dehumanizing obligatory rule of celibacy. Although there will always be a place for celibacy in the Church, its relevance to Latin American culture is seriously questioned. Most Latin American men feel that it is impossible for a man to be a man and not be married. The almost complete lack of communication between men and priest can in very large part be traced to this mistrust of anyone who claims to be a celibate and still be a man. . . .

"Vocations suffer immensely due to the at present necessary practice in local seminaries to view the applicant, not so much as to his love of people and of God, but rather 'can he remain celibate.' A very large number of major seminarians are dropped for this reason. With easily remembered exceptions, the generous, hospitable, God-loving, warmly human characteristics of the Latin personality are strangely absent among the clergy."

In 1965 eighty priests, two bishops, and several theologians met in Buenos Aires to discuss the acute shortage of clergy. They concluded their discussion with a strong recommendation to terminate compulsory celibacy. In a statement prepared for the Second Vatican Council, Bishop Peter Kopp of Brazil declared: "We have to make a choice right away: either to multiply the number of priests, both celibate and married, or look forward to the collapse of the Church in South America." Once again the question boils down to this: Is the retention of compulsory celibacy, of which neither Christ nor the Apostles ever heard, worth the loss of hundreds of millions of souls?

A survey conducted by Father Joseph Fichter, S.J., of Harvard University, disclosed that 62 percent of the rank and file priests in the

United States believe that diocesan priests should have freedom of choice between marriage and celibacy. Most of those who favor such freedom think the choice should be open both before and after ordination. Furthermore, the survey showed that an overwhelming majority —92 percent—agreed that priests who have left the ministry and married should be allowed to return to the sacraments and remain with their wives.

In a far-ranging interview with Father Yves Congar, O.P., a *peritus* at the council and one of the framers of the Dogmatic Constitution on the Church, published in *America,* he was asked by Father Patrick Granfield, O.S.B., if he would favor granting permission to priests to marry after ordination in certain cases. "I would say," he replied, "that permission may be occasionally given for priests to marry. Some men discover the question of sexuality after their ordination, when they are in their late thirties."

He also added: "We must not forget that priestly celibacy is a Church law and not a divine law. There is no theological difference between a married priest, as in the East, and an unmarried priest. Both are priests in the full sense." He predicted that within twenty years "we will have a married clergy in the sense that the Church will ordain married men."

Robbing the Cradle

Father Congar's observation about some men not discovering the truth about their sexual nature until after their ordination is a timely and valid one. Take the case of boys, taken at the age of thirteen and fourteen from their families and sent to a minor and then a major seminary and kept there till ordination. What do they know of their sexual nature, its power, persistence, and dynamism, about marriage and the conjugal life? In what position are they to make a lifelong commitment, abdicating the use of their sexual endowment in any manner whatsoever? We speak about their making a free, deliberate, solemn promise. But how can they be said to be free when they know virtually nothing about love, marriage, the conjugal life, or the joys of parenthood?

"When I entered the minor seminary," related a priest, "the superior said to us: 'Remember that from now on girls and women are to have no place in your thoughts or lives. As far as you are concerned, they simply don't exist.' Before leaving for the summer vacation we were warned to steer completely clear of them and never be alone in their presence."

Isn't this brainwashing with a vengeance? Isn't it robbing the cradle? How much longer can it be tolerated, if the candidate for the priesthood is to have the knowledge and freedom necessary to make an intelligent and truly human decision? Is it any wonder that the enrollment in our seminaries has fallen to an all-time low and resignations from the ministry have risen to an all-time high?

Vatican Council II has brought into the Church a fresh Pentecostal spirit of freedom, honesty, candor, and dedication to truth. This entails the freedom of asking questions. In ever-increasing numbers seminarians and priests are asking the questions just mentioned and they are demanding honest answers.

At the Immaculate Conception Seminary in Conception, Missouri, the students on the college level voted 143 to 32 in favor of optional celibacy instead of compulsory, while those in theology favored optional celibacy by a vote of 65 to 20. The students at a large seminary in the East, not named in the Catholic press release, favored the "right of priests to marry" by a 90 percent vote.

THE MAJOR CONSIDERATION

Perhaps the major consideration which should prompt a reconsideration of the celibacy requirement is the profound and far-reaching change which has occurred in recent years in the Church's thinking concerning marriage and specifically the conjugal act. If Jerome, Ambrose, Augustine, Thomas Aquinas, or virtually any of the Fathers and Doctors of the Church were to read the *Pastoral Constitution on the Church in the Modern World* and especially the sections on the sanctity of marriage and the family and on conjugal love, they would see little resemblance in it to their own writings. Instead of looking upon marriage as a second-rate calling and marital intercourse as a shameful concession to animal lust, justifiable only by procreative intent, the council proclaimed the nobility of the married state and the sanctifying and enriching character of the conjugal act, totally independent of procreation.

"Thus a man and woman," says the council, "who by the marriage covenant of conjugal love 'are no longer two, but one flesh' (Matt.

19:6), render mutual help and service to each other through an intimate union of their persons and of their actions. Through this union they experience the meaning of their oneness and attain to it with growing perfection day by day . . . Christ the Lord abundantly blessed this many-faceted love, welling up as it does from the fountain of divine love and structured as it is on the model of His union with the Church."

The council depicts married love and its distinctive expression as beautiful, holy, enriched with divine love, and leading the spouses to God. "Authentic married love," it says, "is caught up into divine love and is governed and enriched by Christ's redeeming power and the saving activity of the Church. Thus this love can lead the spouses to God with powerful effect and can aid and strengthen them in the sublime office of being a father or a mother."

Conjugal love, points out the council, is not merely physical but is eminently human, and "involves the good of the whole person. Therefore it can enrich the expressions of body and mind with a unique dignity, ennobling these expressions as special ingredients and signs of the friendship distinctive of marriage. This love the Lord has judged worthy of special gifts, healing, perfecting, and exalting gifts of grace and charity."

Here then is an authentic statement of the Church's teaching on marriage and conjugal love. It is the culmination of more than nineteen centuries of growth and development. With Vatican Council's statement before them, what group of churchmen would wish to deny to priests or bishops the right to such a sacrament to assist them not only in living upright and holy lives but also in achieving sainthood? Fortified with the companionship, counsel, prayers, and love of a devoted helpmate, may not a priest be better enabled to be a model for his flock and a more understanding, dedicated, and Christlike shepherd of souls?

This does not mean that marriage is to be thrust upon anyone. There will always be a place—and an honorable one—in the ministry for the celibate priest. It simply means that the basic human right and fundamental freedom of every man to decide for himself will be respected.

Pope John XXIII, as all the world knows, had a remarkable gift of reading the signs of the times and thus perceiving developments while still in their embryological form. With remarkable clarity he perceived the inarticulate groping, hoping, yearning, and craving of vast numbers of young priests to be relieved of the agonizing burden of compulsory celibacy that they might live normal, happy, holy lives in the pastoral ministry.

In a conversation with his old friend, Professor Etienne Gilson, in 1963, His Holiness said: "Do you want me to tell you what is my greatest worry? I do not mean as a human being, but as a pope. I am continuously vexed by the thought of those young priests who so courageously carry the burden of ecclesiastical celibacy. For some among them it is a martyrdom. Yes, a kind of martyrdom. It often seems to me that I hear a sort of complaint—from here, but from much farther—as if voices were asking the Church to take that burden away from them."

In his encyclical *The Development of People,* Pope Paul VI gave timely expression to a truth of worldwide importance today. "Where the inalienable right to marriage and procreation is lacking," declared His Holiness, "human dignity has ceased to exist." That statement reflects the conviction of every nation in the civilized world, and it is difficult to conceive of any intelligent person taking issue with it. When the Church implements that statement in its own life, the teaching and practice of compulsory celibacy for priests will have ceased to exist.

15

TIME FOR A CHANGE

by John A. O'Brien

On June 24, 1967, Pope Paul VI issued the encyclical *Priestly Celibacy* to "his bishops, to his brothers in the priesthood, and to the faithful of the entire Catholic world." Many were surprised that the encyclical was issued prior to the convening of the Synod of Bishops in Rome in September for a discussion of the problems confronting the Church today.

The encyclical speaks beautifully of the dignity and sanctity of the priesthood and extols celibacy to the skies. While the document tries to speak sympathetically of "the sweet burden of sacerdotal chastity," it does nothing to relieve that burden, which countless thousands of priests are finding almost unbearable and a constant source of pain and agony.

The encyclical invites study and explicitly urges that we "look openly at the principal objections against the law of celibacy." "Far from putting an end to discussion of the subject," says an editorial in *America,* "the encyclical will give a new orientation and fresh stimulus to dialogue . . . As long as *Priestly Celibacy* remains an utterance of the Pope alone, it will not bear its intended fruit in a Church that is both Roman and Catholic."

The encyclical cites some of the objections to compulsory celibacy, but it presents them in an exceedingly abbreviated form, which does not at all reflect their strength or cogency. Many theologians, biblical scholars, psychologists, and Church historians regret that it does not reflect the new currents of thought and insight opened up by modern research in these respective disciplines. The objections are put up like men of straw, only to be knocked down with a flourish.

The document is especially disappointing in four other respects:

1. It does not distinguish with sufficient clarity the difference between a vocation to the priesthood and the vocation to virginity. It brings no comfort, insight, or help to the priest who has a call to the priesthood but has no call to virginity.

2. It does not bring out with sufficient clarity and candor the prevalence of a married priesthood in the early Church and for many centuries afterward, nor does it acknowledge that there were approximately forty popes who were married legally and validly.

3. The document, approving continued practice of compulsory celibacy as a condition for the priesthood, does not square with the great principle enunciated by Pope Paul VI in the encyclical *The Development of People*, quoted in the previous chapter: "Where the inalienable right to marriage and procreation is lacking, human dignity has ceased to exist." If priests are human beings, it is difficult to see how they can be denied their inalienable right to marriage and procreation.

4. The encyclical does not acknowledge the clear unmistakable fact that the linkage of perpetual bachelorhood to the priesthood lies at the heart of the shortage of priests and seminarians, causing untold millions of souls to be lost from the Church today.

The fatal flaw in the whole document is, in the judgment of many impartial scholars, the crucial failure to distinguish between two separate and distinct vocations of priesthood and virginity. This leads to the arbitrary and unfortunate disciplinary ruling which requires a promise of lifelong bachelorhood to become a priest.

Shortly after the issuance of the encyclical I was in correspondence with two noted Catholic scholars concerning the linkage of bachelorhood with priesthood and the need for discussing it openly. One was Father Yves Congar who wrote me: "I am certainly in agreement with you in thinking that the encyclical has not said the last word on this question. It does not respond in a completely satisfactory way to the question that it raises, namely the gap between the vocation to the ministry and the vocation to celibacy. That is the essential question."

The other was His Beatitude Maximos IV Saigh, Melkite Patriarch of Antioch and of all the East, and a Roman cardinal. In a letter dated September 3, 1967, he told me of an intervention, or talk, which he had prepared to give at Vatican Council II but was prevented by the Pope's order forbidding such public discussion. In his prepared talk he urged that celibacy be not made a condition for ordination in the Latin rite Church on the grounds that a man may have a vocation to the priesthood but not to lifelong bachelorhood.

"Our conclusions," he wrote to me, "retain their validity even after the publication of the recent encyclical of the pope on ecclesiastical celibacy. There is no doubt that celibacy 'for the sake of the kingdom' is possible, desirable, and even superior to marriage. *But is it necessary that it be a condition obligatory and sine qua non for the priesthood? There alone lies the question.* One could continue to speak forever about the dignity of celibacy and its advantages. But that is not where the difficulty lies."

His Beatitude informed me that after the council he forwarded to the Pope a copy of his prepared intervention along with an accompanying letter. In the letter he stated: "In regard to the Latin clergy, all that I propose to lay before Your Holiness is the wish that Your Holiness would set up a commission in order to study this problem in open discussion. Holy Father, this problem exists and is becoming more difficult from day to day. It demands a solution. It is useless to close our eyes to this problem or consider it taboo. Your Holiness knows very well that truths on which silence is maintained turn to poison. . . .

"Celibacy will always remain the ideal of an elite which God chooses for Himself and which never dies out. But that is no reason why celibacy should be imposed as an indispensable condition for the priesthood. If secular priests are not required to practice monastic poverty, which is much easier to observe, why are they forced into celibacy, which is certainly a very special vocation and demands very special dispositions? . . . all that I ask of Your Holiness, in order to follow a serious call of conscience, is that the door should not be systematically and irrevocably closed."

The planned intervention and accompanying letter sent to His Holiness are models of clear thinking, lucid expression, and cogent reasoning. They glow with a burning love of the Church and the priesthood and a deep concern for the future of the Latin rite Church, if provision is not made to permit men to become priests without robbing them of their inalienable right to marriage and procreation. While too long to be quoted in full in this chapter, these important documents are presented in the Appendix along with other material of great moment, which every reader will do well to peruse.

Another topic which demands discussion is the unconscionable slowness of the Roman officials in acting upon the petitions of priests for dispensation from celibacy. Many, probably most, do not want to be reduced to the lay state, but simply wish to marry and continue as good, devoted, and holy priests. The Church needs them. The laity needs them.

Supplementing the celibate ministers, these priests will bring a new vitality to the Church and a new competence to their dealing with family problems. Indeed one cannot but wonder if the birth-control problem, now shaking the Church to its very foundations, would even exist if many of our priests, bishops, cardinals, and even the Pope as well were married men.

When priests apply for the dispensation, they wait and wait and wait. Month after month rolls by, and their appeal remains unanswered. One of the contributors informs me that he has been waiting for twenty-two months for a reply to his application for laicization. Some have been kept waiting for years. This is Rome's method of torturing them.

In probably no other institution on the face of the earth will one find the inconsiderateness, harshness, and cruelty which characterizes Rome's dealing with priests who humbly beg release from the celibacy which, they feel, is corroding their whole lives and causing them untold anguish. That they have given five, ten, fifteen, or twenty years of devoted service, with meager pay for men of their training, seems to bring no expression of gratitude from the Church.

When employees of a professional class—as priests are—terminate their employment with a business firm after years of service, they are showered with expressions of gratitude, honor, and affection and generally provided with a generous pension for life. How shabby, in contrast, is the treatment customarily meted out to priests. They are treated as renegades, derelicts, and almost as criminals. Some are required to see psychiatrists. Everything possible is done to humiliate, hurt, and torture them.

Here one perceives a persistence of the spirit of incredible cruelty which characterized the Holy Roman Inquisition established by Pope Gregory IX in February 1231. While the persecution of heretics had been going on for a century, it was Gregory who put it on an organized systematic basis with his publication of the constitution *Excommunicatus*. This decreed life imprisonment as a "salutary" punishment for repentant heretics and capital punishment for obstinate heretics after their surrender to the secular arm.

The common method of executing such heretics was burning them at the stake. When at times the civil ruler was reluctant or slow to carry out such an inhuman sentence, the Pope would threaten him with excommunication and removal from office. Yet the only crime of which the heretic was guilty was in remaining faithful to the dictates of his own conscience, which was not only his right but also his duty. Thus did the Roman Church trample upon its own teaching to satisfy its lust for vengeance.

The practice of persecuting, torturing, and burning witnesses was recommended and doctrinally justified by Innocent IV in an authoritative encyclical. In 1311 the Council of Vienna decreed that theologians who endeavored in any way to justify usury, or the charging of interest on money loaned, were to be "imprisoned in iron chains" for the rest of their lives. This warning was carried in moral theology textbooks published in Italy as late as the eighteenth century, when the doctrine was added to the growing scrap heap of other discarded doctrines long insisted upon by popes.

Not only were the penalties atrocious, but the methods of procedure in trying the accused were shocking as well. Due process of law, the right to confront his accusers, to have counsel and to present witnesses in his own defense, and other elementary requirements of justice were commonly or frequently denied. Even the heretic who recanted after the death sentence had been pronounced, far from being cleared, was sentenced to life imprisonment in solitary confinement.

The Church's lust for vengeance, however, was not satisfied with life imprisonment or death. The condemned were denied Christian burial and their bodies were often exhumed and burned. For six centuries, from the twelfth to the eighteenth, the Church displayed a wanton disregard for elementary human rights and for the dignity of the person, and an implacable savagery toward all who disagreed with its teachings, that blacken its name with an infamy which a thousand centuries will be unable to erase.

The torture-stained record of the "Holy Inquisition" still shocks the reader of today and makes him wonder how an institution which claims to speak in the name of the gentle and compassionate Christ could be guilty of such horrible and atrocious cruelty and vengeance. Much of it stems from a total disregard for the elementary right of a person to follow his own conscience in matters of religious belief as long as he does not thereby inflict harm upon society.

Because of its cruelty, utter disregard for elementary human rights, and hostility to the spirit of scientific and theological inquiry, the Inquisition has come to be a symbol of cruelty, intellectual terrorism, and religious intolerance. Misguided Catholic apologists have sought to exonerate the Church for the crimes of the Inquisition, but their efforts have been futile. "The Inquisition," acknowledges *The Catholic Encyclopedia for Home and School*, "not only offends modern ideals of justice and spiritual freedom, it also contradicts the teaching of the fathers and doctors of the Church such as St. Bernard, who said that faith must be 'the result of conviction and should not be imposed by force.'"

It was hoped that the Second Vatican Council's *Declaration on Religious Liberty*, guaranteeing to every person the right of religious belief and freedom of conscience, would put an end to efforts at coercion. But threats emanating from Rome and from individual bishops to apply sanctions to those who in some cases are unable in conscience to follow the directives of the non-infallible *Humanae Vitae* encyclical, are profoundly disturbing. That is why the noted moral theologian, Bernard Häring, sounded a timely warning in reminding us of the excesses of the Inquisition and the need of the theologians and other scholars for liberty to express their honest convictions.

The "Holy Inquisition" and "holy wars" could have been erased from the picture of the Church, he points out, if "the prophetic spirit and the courage to speak out openly with Christian freedom had been more highly valued in the Church. When the popes and their curial theologians so frequently and so emphatically defended temporal power and the Vatican States as a divinely commissioned right and a spiritual necessity, this critical Christian frankness should have been more in evidence." What is needed today is for all in the Church to speak out openly against the little clique of reactionaries pushing the Pope back to the worldly narrowness exemplified in the *Syllabus of Errors* and the Church's prohibition of Italians from voting in their own country, which lasted from 1870 to 1929.

The name of the Holy Roman Inquisition was changed to the Sacred Congregation of Roman and Universal Inquisition by Pope Paul III on July 21, 1542, and later by Pope St. Pius X to the Congregation of the Holy Office. Though the name was changed, the persecuting spirit of the original inquisitors remained essentially the same.

The Congregation was still the accuser, judge, jury, sheriff, and executioner combined. It remained in the eyes of scholars as a symbol of intellectual terrorism and suppression of any fresh thinking. Theologians, philosophers, and scriptural scholars, who did not know that the Holy Office was even aware of their existence, suddenly found themselves condemned for allegedly unorthodox views. In consequence Catholic biblical studies lagged a full decade or more behind those of Protestant scholars.

Deploring its medieval and high-handed tactics, Cardinal Frings of Cologne reflected the mind of virtually all the Fathers of Vatican Council II when he declared: "The methods and behavior of the Congregation of the Holy Office do not conform at all to the modern era and are a cause of scandal to the Church." This was probably the greatest understatement made during the whole council.

All hope of achieving the updating, for which the council was summoned, was doomed as long as the Holy Office, dominated by Cardinal Ottaviani, persisted in its procedures. Aware of this and of the worldwide scorn of it, Pope Paul VI on December 7, 1965, established new procedures and changed its name to the Sacred Congregation for the Doctrine of the Faith. Though no longer the pro-prefect, Cardinal Ottaviani is still a member and his influence is still said to be dominant.

Unfortunately this is the congregation of the Roman Curia, with which priests seeking release from the celibacy obligation must deal.

They are finding in its tortuous slowness and reluctance to act upon their petitions a persistence of the spirit of repression, harshness, and vengeance which has characterized this inquisitorial body through the centuries. It is not easy for the leopard to change its spots. Neither is it easy for an organization of inquisitors, long accustomed to repression and persecution, to change its spirit or its tactics.

The grievance most frequently voiced by priests seeking release from the celibacy obligation is the dilatory tactics of the Congregation. Months and even years go by without an answer. The purpose is apparently to frustrate the applicant and torture him, thinking that this will drive from his mind any thought of escaping from the perpetual bachelorhood in which he feels imprisoned.

Snail-like slowness of action is not confined to the Congregation for the Doctrine of the Faith, but seems to be characteristic of the Roman Curia as a whole. The Sacred Roman Rota is a tribunal of the Roman Curia which handles marriage cases. To illustrate its slowness we cite a damage suit that was brought against it by Melchiorre Palermo, fifty-seven, of Trapani, Italy, in September 1967. He was asking for compensation of several hundred thousand lira for "material and moral damages." What had the Sacred Roman Rota done to him? It had merely kept him waiting for twenty years before acting upon his petition for a declaration of the nullity of his marriage.

As reported in the world's press, Palermo was surprised in Rosa Conforto's home in 1944 by her relatives and three policemen. The girl was eighteen. He was arrested for presumed rape, but the charge was dropped automatically according to Italian law practice when he accepted the proposal of the girl's family and married her in the jail's chapel. Upon being released, Palermo immediately filed suit with a local Church court to have the marriage annulled on the grounds of lack of true consent, since he simply wanted to escape from a long confinement in prison.

After a couple of years the case was referred to the Rota where it remained on its docket for twenty years before it handed down the decision that Palermo's marriage was null. In his suit for damages he charged that the Rota had kept him committed to a marriage whose deficiency of consent appeared clear from the beginning, thus "impeding me from building a family on the moral and civil foundations guaranteed by the constitution to all Italian citizens." The case illustrates vividly the gross injustice and cruelty inflicted upon an individual by the failure of a court to act with reasonable promptness.

This is a common grievance among priests seeking relief from the celibacy obligation. Few, if any, priests would petition for such action without first giving serious and careful consideration. A further wait of three or even four months is understandable, but dragging it out for eight, nine, ten months and even a year or more is difficult to justify. It then takes on the aspects of inconsiderateness and harshness.

As a result of the unconscionable slowness of processing applications for release from celibacy there is now a backlog of more than 4,000 cases awaiting action in Rome. Think of all the dedicated manpower, so desperately needed today, which is being lost through failure to dispense them from the man-made law of celibacy and allow them to continue their priestly ministry. Here is a case of an apparent willingness to let the Church virtually collapse rather than modernize its outmoded legislation on this subject.

There is moreover a growing consensus that the law requiring such dispensation ceases to bind under such circumstances. The principle in theology called *epikeia* expressly states that a law does not apply or bind when its application would work a hardship not intended by the legislator. As a consequence an ever-increasing number of priests are no longer applying, but are simply contracting marriage before a civil magistrate, a non-Catholic minister, an Orthodox priest, or a friendly and understanding Catholic priest who shares the same conviction.

The common procedure for laicization requires the priest to be married first by a justice of the peace, usually in a place where he is not known. Then a priest designated by the chancery office marries him in a church, usually late at night, with no witnesses. He does not enter the marriage in the parish matrimonial register nor send a notice of it to the parish church in which the married priest was baptized, as is normally done. Everything possible is done to keep it supersecret on the grounds that it would disedify the people.

But such grounds no longer obtain. During the year 1968 priests in the United States have been marrying on the average of two a day. For several years this has been going on, and it has been reported in the press so often that it scarcely ranks any longer as newsworthy. Religious order priests as well as diocesan ones—pastors, assistants, seminary and college professors, rectors, and chancery officials—have been marrying while others are publicly announcing each day their intention to do so.

Marriage is a sacrament which showers blessings upon its recipients and leads them into an honorable and holy state. Why, then, should it not be entered into with dignity and joy in the presence of one's friends and relatives? Why make it a furtive affair as if it were some criminal act? Would it not be much better for all concerned to have the marriage take place at a Nuptial Mass with beautiful music and song and with the bridal party and their many friends receiving our Eucharistic Lord?

This would be the honest and decent thing to do, and it would make it easy for the married priest to continue his priestly ministry with the respect, esteem, and love of his people. The overwhelming majority of our laity is now ready for this, as the latest polls show. Nothing but an increase of grace and of love for God and neighbor can result from the reception of matrimony, which St. Paul so aptly called "a great sacrament."

"Father," remarked an American bishop to me, "it would be much better if Rome would authorize every bishop to handle the petitions of any of his priests for dispensation from celibacy. He knows them and can readily decide what is best for the Church and the priest concerned. The functionary in Rome who handles the case and is called upon to decide has little more than the name of the applicant on a piece of paper before him.

"There it remains," he continued, "for an unconscionably long time. When he finally decides, he knows little, if any more, than when the petition first arrived. This is not an intelligent or efficient way of acting and it must be changed as soon as possible before greater harm befalls the Church."

With this constructive suggestion of a leading American bishop, most every Catholic will agree. It is but one of the many steps that must be taken to deal intelligently and effectively with one of the most urgent problems facing the Church not only in the United States but also in virtually every country in the world: the revamping of the legislation so that priests may either withdraw from the ministry with dignity and honor to take up other work, or to marry and continue in the active ministry as a good, dedicated, and holy married priest.

The additional sacrament which he receives will not lessen his capacity to serve, but is more likely to increase it. The love of a help-mate will not diminish his love for his people or his God but will give it a new ardor, a new depth, and a greater intensity. This is the direction in which the Church must travel if it is to continue and grow and bring peace, happiness, and the love of God to a worried and confused world which stands so desperately in need of them today.

APPENDIX

1

PRELATES, PRIESTS MEET
Celibacy Included in U.S. Study

Detroit (NC)—A major study on the life of priests being made by the bishops of the United States will include the question of celibacy, according to a joint announcement from the office of Archbishop John F. Dearden of Detroit and the officers of the National Association for Pastoral Renewal (NAPR).

NAPR is an organization of priests and lay persons formed primarily to promote the idea that celibacy should be optional—not mandatory—for Catholic priests. Last December its officers cabled Pope Paul VI asking him to permit "further discussion" of clerical celibacy and to "make it possible for those men who honorably wish to leave the priesthood to do so with dignity." NAPR has frequently charged the United States bishops with refusing to discuss the celibacy issue.

The National Conference of Catholic Bishops (NCCB), at its annual meeting in Washington, D.C., last fall, reaffirmed the value of celibacy and declared it would be "irresponsible on our part to hold out any hope that this discipline will be changed. Such expectation is without foundation," the bishops added.

The NCCB then announced a detailed program for the study on the life and ministry of priests, under the Bishops' Committee on Pastoral Research and Practices headed by Cardinal John Krol of Philadelphia.

Recently, Archbishop Dearden, who is president of the NCCB, and Bishop Alexander M. Zaleski of Lansing, vice chairman of the NCCB committee undertaking the study, met in Detroit with a group of NAPR officers, including the president, Father Thomas Pucelik of Lincoln, Neb.

"The discussion centered around the present study that is being made by a number of scholars," according to the joint announcement. "Its purpose is to define the role and meaning of the contemporary priesthood.

"Since the study will be of a scholarly nature, all aspects of priestly life will be considered including celibacy. It was emphasized that the study will be objective, with its conclusions in no way predetermined. The cooperation of individuals or organizations, such as the NAPR, will be welcomed by those involved in the study."

The announcement said there was also discussion at the meeting of problems relating to the process of laicization for priests who wish to leave the ministry. "Both the officers of the NAPR and the bishops expressed their concern for priests who for reasons of conscience have decided to leave the ministry."

St. Louis Review, St. Louis, Mo.
April 12, 1968

2

CABLEGRAM SENT TO POPE PAUL VI
December 18, 1967

**By Rev. Allen E. Carter, Vice-President,
National Association for Pastoral Renewal
P.O. Box 584, Madison Square Station, New York, N.Y. 10010**

Confident that Your Holiness will be open to our appeal, we write to you as men who have a deep love and concern for the Church. The

National Association for Pastoral Renewal which we represent has concerned itself with the pastoral problems associated with the present discipline of priestly celibacy in the Western Church. Since our inception one year ago we have tried to work, and we shall continue to work, within the spirit and essential structures of the Church. We were inspired with hope by the words of the Vatican Council: "The relationships between the Bishop and his diocesan priests should rest above all upon the bonds of supernatural charity so that harmony of the will of the priests with that of their bishop will render their pastoral activity more fruitful. Hence for the sake of greater service to souls, let the Bishop engage in discussion with his priests, even collectively, especially about pastoral matters." (On Bishops, #28.)

We have appealed repeatedly to our Bishops to enter into Christian dialogue with us on pastoral questions relating to celibacy. Of 850 letters of appeal, only 12 were even afforded the courtesy of an acknowledgment; none produced the desired dialogue. Apparently we have been classified by our Bishops as among those who, they say, "give the impression of not only challenging established discipline but of rejecting values that touch our Catholic beliefs to the scandal of the faithful and with notable detriment to vocations." (Bishops' statement on Clerical Celibacy, November 1967.)

This has caused great disillusionment among our members, who include laymen, religious, and diocesan priests. It seems so far removed from the "readiness to listen" and "trusting familiarity" recommended to the Bishops in the Council. (On Bishops, #16.) We do not feel that our position favoring optional celibacy makes us any less Catholic than the Eastern Churches who have long acknowledged the compatibility of the sacrament of Orders and the sacrament of Matrimony. Without in any way denigrating the brilliant jewel that celibacy can be, we acknowledge with the Vatican Council that celibacy "is not, indeed, demanded by the very nature of the priesthood, as is evident from the practice of the primitive Church and from the tradition of the Eastern Churches." (On Priests, #16.) To treat this appeal with disdain and threats of discrimination because of our position on this matter is an implied slight to our Eastern Catholic brethren, as some of them have noted with sadness. It is also an insult to our integrity.

No one could say or has said that all the questions relative to compulsory priestly celibacy have been answered to the satisfaction of all concerned. The question, therefore, requires further discussion. We would like this discussion to exemplify the words of the Council's Declaration on Religious Freedom: "Truth, however, is to be sought after in a manner proper to the dignity of the human person and his social nature. The inquiry is to be free, carried on with the aid of teaching or instruction, communication and dialogue." Otherwise the Church has a double standard: one which it preaches to the world and another which it enforces within the Church. The Church is less credible for this.

Even if it should be determined without genuine dialogue that the discipline of celibacy will not be altered, we cannot ignore the injustice and scandalous lack of compassion inflicted on those priests who, with fidelity to their consciences, decide to leave the active priesthood and marry. Although no policy has been publicly formulated, the practice, as Your Holiness must know, is that men, with few exceptions, are not allowed to marry in the Church with the comforts of the liturgy until they have married civilly and thus contracted the canonical penalty of excommunication. Even then, they are required in many instances to wait indefinitely long periods and then are married in a secrecy that is utterly suggestive of disgrace and lacking in the joy that should accompany the Christian sacraments. The Church has recognized in practice and in law that solemn vows can, in various ways, cease to bind. Why should the obligation of priestly celibacy be treated as more binding? Surely a priest who judges that celibacy is not conducive to his personal and spiritual well-being should not be penalized and denied dignified and reasonable access to sacramental marriage.

The manner in which those priests who request a dispensation from celibacy are treated shows so little humanity, so little love, so little willingness to accord them the dignity of their priesthood, that it constitutes a major scandal. You are in a position to change this and we beg you, in God's name, to do so.

The evolution of any society in its slow and painful rise from barbarism can be measured in the relationship of the person to the community. It is only to a primitive and embattled society that the free exercise of rights is ever a threat; it is only a primitive and fear-ridden society that submerges the individual to community goals with gross and disproportionate sanctions.

Like yourself, we desire the Church to exist before men as a society knit together by self-giving love. We want the Church to be an example of justice, mercy, and compassion. The inhumane treatment of priests who wish to leave the priestly service is becoming more and more of a scandal. We ask you to make it possible for those men who honorably wish to leave the priesthood to do so with dignity.

3

THE ENCYCLICAL ON CELIBACY DOES NOT SOLVE THE PROBLEM

Tübingen, Germany (DPA). Asked about the importance of Paul VI's encyclical on celibacy, Dr. Hans Küng, the Catholic theologian from Tübingen, replied:

"The service done by the encyclical is to bring the difficulties about celibacy to open discussion. It does not resolve the problem, but sharpens it in giving expression to it. The Gospel knows of a personal call to individuals to celibacy for the service of men, and Jesus and Paul by living thus gave an example even for our own time. But Jesus and Paul alike expressly guaranteed full freedom to each individual.

"Now a general law of celibacy is opposed to this expressly guaranteed freedom of celibacy as a free charism. Peter and the Apostles were, and stayed, married even in the full discipleship of Jesus, and this remained the pattern for the leaders of the community for many subsequent centuries. But what had its original freely chosen place, mainly in monastic communities, was in later centuries extended as an express prohibition of marriage to the clergy generally and was in part imposed on them.

"In our conciliar and post-conciliar time, however, the opinion is growing even inside the Catholic Church, among clergy and laity, that this extremely restrictive legal invasion of personal human rights offends not only the primitive free constitution of the Church but also contemporary understanding of individual freedom.

"In today's state of the Church three problems especially require solution, raised by the present regulations of canon law:

"1. The Church is losing in recent years an alarmingly growing number of often highly qualified candidates for the priesthood, whom it needs now more than ever.

"2. The number of those who later leave the service of the Church or incur unavoidable difficulties by unfaithfulness in their duties, goes into the tens of thousands (four thousand applications from priests for legitimate dispensations are now before the Roman Curia; in Italy alone, however, the number of priests who have left without dispensation is currently between six and fifteen thousand; no statistics have been published.)

"3. In view of the rather enormous lack of priests and the well-known aging of the clergy, the question whether to marry or not must be referred to the *primary* commitment of the Church in order above all to give leaders to the community.

"Other arguments could be discussed. In any case there will be no rest about this matter in the Catholic Church until celibacy is again, as it was originally, left to the free decision of the individual, and until then, under conditions we can only guess at, is retroactively introduced into Canon Law."

For further progress Küng advocated the *collegial* treatment of the problem in the episcopal synod due to meet in Rome during the fall. Conciliar discussion was, as is known, prevented. Collegiality in the Church also requires, Küng pointed out, that the priests concerned should themselves be asked in secret ballot whether they prefer a *law* of celibacy, or that celibacy should be left to the *decision of the individual*.

4

SAIGH'S APPEAL ON CELIBACY

During the fourth session of the Second Vatican Council Pope Paul VI specifically banned formal discussion by the council Fathers of priestly celibacy. As a result, an intervention on the topic which had been prepared by the Melkite Patriarch Maximos IV Saigh, who died Nov. 5, 1967, was never delivered. The text of the Patriarch's intervention has now been published in the German publication *Der Seelsorger,* and an English translation appeared in the *Tablet,* London. Also published was a covering letter sent by Maximos in transmitting his intervention to the Pope. The texts are published here with the permission of the *Tablet.*

Venerable Fathers: The text put before us on "the office and life of the priest" devotes a paragraph (#16) to the "evangelical counsels in the life of the priest," that is, to perfect chastity, poverty and obedience.

Where the chastity of the priest is mentioned, the text stresses the advantages of celibacy.

Nothing would be finer, more correct and more necessary than to emphasize the importance of celibacy, its suitability for the priestly state, its ascetic and apostolic advantages, especially today, when celibacy is the object of unjust attacks.

In fact, virginity and celibacy for the sake of the kingdom of God are two eminent priestly virtues which mark out the Church with a halo and exalt still more her radiance and her redeeming action. Christ and His mother are perfect examples of these virtues. Although the council has extolled the dignity of the family and conjugal love, it remains true none the less that the voluntary acceptance of celibacy is the supreme sign of a life wholly dedicated to God. On this the whole tradition of the Church, East and West, is agreed.

If however the beauty of the celibate priesthood is emphasized, this should not mean the destruction and disdaining of the parallel and equally apostolic tradition of a priesthood which has taken on itself the bonds of holy matrimony—as we have encountered it and still encounter it today in the Eastern Church. By married priests we mean men already married who can become priests, but not men already ordained as priests who want to marry: for, according to both Eastern and Western tradition, ordination to the priesthood places a man firmly in his state of life.

If they read paragraph 16, married men in the Eastern Church and the very rare cases in the Western Church—who are just as Catholic as the others—will inevitably gain the impression that their priesthood is merely tolerated or is an emergency solution. But this is by no means the case. The conciliar text must rise to such a high plane of catholicity that it embraces all situations.

Permit me, venerable Fathers, to put before you briefly the spiritual and apostolic advantages presented by a married clergy as it exists in the Eastern Church. I am convinced that in this way I am fulfilling a duty, for it is a question here of a profoundly Catholic institution which cannot be quickly disposed of by a division into two lines as the schema does in paragraph 16. I am fulfilling this duty for your information. The

Christian West is free to adopt the development which accords better with its temperament and what it holds to be in the interest of the Church. But as in a number of other points, the Christian East also has maintained for the benefit of the universal Church a parallel tradition, which is founded no less than the other tradition on Scripture, the Apostles, and the Fathers of the Church. And, at this time and in the countries where the Catholic Church considers it opportune, an appeal might be made to this tradition in order to underpin a turning point in history, a turning point which will perhaps become necessary through the changing circumstances of times, places and persons.

We offer the following considerations:

1. Neither Scripture nor Tradition, particularly that of the first centuries, regards celibacy as an indispensable condition for the priesthood, as a *conditio sine qua non.* In the original text of the schema it is stated: "Even among the apostles some were married." In the new text it was thought fit to omit this observation, as if this omission could alter the historical truth. We have no need to recall the fact that St. Peter and the first disciples were married. Those in the Eastern Church who today are also married deserve our complete respect.

2. The East makes a clear distinction between priesthood and monasticism. It is possible to have a vocation to one without having a vocation to the other. This distinction opens new perspectives: celibacy is the specific vocation of the monk; it is not necessarily the specific vocation of the priest as minister of the Church. Priesthood is more a function than a state of life. It is not linked with personal perfection, as celibacy is for God, but for the benefit of the Church. Celibacy therefore can disappear, if it is to the advantage of ecclesiastical office. The mystery of redemption, which is continued in the priesthood, is not subject to any particular form. In case of necessity priesthood must not be sacrificed to celibacy, but celibacy to the priesthood.

3. These distinctions between priestly vocation and vocation to the monastic life existed from the first Christian centuries and were based on an idealistic moral severity. At the Council of Nicaea (325) the council Fathers tried to impose complete continence on the married clergy. If we can believe Socrates the historian, St. Paphnutius, Bishop of Thebes, confessor of the faith and miracle-worker, generally known for his chastity and his strict morality, defended with common sense and realism the traditional institution of the married priesthood. And

all the Fathers of the council, so the historian records, accepted this judgment. Since then the Oriental Church has remained loyal to this tradition, which fosters celibacy but does not make it compulsory. The Western Church followed another tradition, until finally she prescribes celibacy definitively and universally at the First Lateran Council (1123): a tradition which in spite of everything only came to prevail at a very late date.

4. However that may be, it is certain that the Oriental tradition produces very numerous priestly vocations, such as the Church needs particularly today. The lack of priests—which is observed with anxiety in our modern times, particularly in certain countries—cannot be satisfied by inadequate palliatives, no matter how important these may be, such as the loan of priests from dioceses in a favorable situation.

5. Moreover, there are a number of persons who have a great desire to serve the Church and human souls, but are incapable of observing perfect chastity. This holds particularly in certain milieus, where bodily and mental isolation presents a great danger to an average celibate priest.

6. Finally, I would like further to observe that there is no cause for anxiety that the freedom of choice between celibacy and marriage assured by the Eastern Church might gradually lead to the disappearance of ecclesiastical chastity. There are and there always will be in the Church souls with a special vocation to give themselves completely to God. We can find proofs of this in the Eastern Churches, both Catholic and Orthodox, where both categories of priest exist alongside one another, each in their full personal development and in their relative perfection. In this freedom of choice and of commitment we have on the contrary fewer lapses to lament, more virtues to admire.

Another serious consideration: as leaders of the Church we cannot regard without anxiety how Christendom is failing to bring about a conversion of the world, and this as a result of the shortage of priests; for the development of Christianity in the world through births and conversions is far from keeping pace with the vertiginous increase of population. Christianity therefore is constantly falling back, and this relative, continuous reversal comes about with a much more rapid rhythm as the years go by—a fact which must give us much food for thought.

Although I am justifying the Eastern tradition, I cannot but admire the high moral level of the traditional trend in the West. But perhaps the time has come when the tradition of the East, by the will of the Church and where she wills, might be helpful to the whole Church.

I conclude: In view of the fact that minds are not yet ripe for a final decision, we suggest the setting up of a post-conciliar commission for a study of this serious problem which in the most exact sense of the words concerns the life of the Church herself. We believe that a straightforward and simple return to the old and true tradition of the Church would be approved by enlightened Christians and by a clergy open to the realities of life. This would serve the peace of souls and freedom of conscience.

LETTER TO PAUL: THE DOOR SHOULD NOT BE CLOSED

Holy Father: As your Holiness wishes, I hasten to send you, in accordance with the advice of the council presidents, the text of the intervention on the theme of "Priesthood, Marriage, and Celibacy in the Oriental Church," which I wanted to deliver before the council.

My intention was solely to interpret and elucidate the Eastern tradition of married priests. The text of the schema suggested to us uses three lines to dispose of this venerable institution, which goes back to the apostles, as a barely tolerated custom. It seems to me that the text of the schema at this point must be considerably changed. Without such alteration it would amount to an insult to the married clergy in the whole of the Eastern Church, both Catholic and Orthodox.

In regard to the Latin clergy, all that I propose to lay before your Holiness is the wish that your Holiness would set up a commission in order to study this problem in open discussion. Holy Father, this problem exists and is becoming more difficult from day to day. It demands a solution. It is useless to close our eyes to this problem or consider it taboo. Your Holiness knows very well that truths on which silence is maintained turn to poison.

I am completely in agreement with the opinion that a public debate in the council hall would have produced more scandal than concrete results, above all if the press were involved and feelings excited. I am, however, convinced that, in spite of the applause which the directives on this subject received, the problem disturbs the conscience of more than one bishop. We are constantly receiving confidential communications from priests who are otherwise known for their piety and their zeal and who beg us to raise our voice, to break the silence. Alarming statistics are produced. Far too many candidates for the priesthood are held back because of the increasing difficulties of celibacy. Others are driven into it and admitted too easily. A large number of married priests could serve the Church as priests.

Celibacy will always remain the ideal of an elite which God chooses for Himself and which never dies out. But that is no reason why celibacy should be imposed as an indispensable condition for the priest- hood. If secular priests are not required to practice monastic poverty, which is much easier to observe, why are they forced into celibacy, which is certainly a very special vocation and demands very special dispositions?

The Catholic West does not yet appear to be ready for such a radical change of discipline. Slowly however it will come to this, with all the caution necessary after the experiment of married deacons, whom the council has already admitted.

All that I ask of your Holiness, in order to follow a serious call of conscience, is that the door will not be systematically and irrevocably closed. With this confidence I humbly kiss your Holiness' hands and beg your fatherly and apostolic blessing.

5

RESOLUTIONS OF THE NATIONAL ASSOCIATION FOR PASTORAL RENEWAL

Adopted at Its Meeting, September 6–8, 1967
At the University of Notre Dame
Notre Dame, Indiana, U.S.A.

With deep concern for the service of the People of God, for the foster- ing of Christian unity; for the recruitment of a clergy now declining in numbers; in recognition of the dignity and freedom of the individual priest and in light of the principle of collegiality, we, the participants in the National Symposium on Clerical Celibacy, held September 6–8, 1967, at Notre Dame, Indiana, support the proposal that diocesan priests of the Latin rite be permitted the option of marrying or remain- ing celibate while exercising the active ministry of the Church. We are persuaded that only through free and genuine choice will the charismatic meaning of virginity be safeguarded, as we hope it will, within the community of Christ. We believe that in this way, optional celibacy will more richly manifest the charity, justice and freedom of Christ, in His Church, and provide a greater opportunity for a priest's personal fulfillment and service to the People of God.

In addressing ourselves to our Bishops about the immediacy of this question, we are fully cognizant of the vast spiritual and sociological problems facing the Church in the modern world. Precisely because of this concern, we feel that individual choice in the matter of celibacy is a prerequisite for a more effective public ministry.

Therefore we urge:

1. That diocesan priests of the Latin rite have the individual option of the celibate or the married state while retaining their active ministry by specifically abrogating canons 132 #1 and 1072.

2. That married priests currently outside the ministry again be permitted to participate in the sacraments; and that, if they so choose, these priests be returned to the active ministry, after due consideration of individual cases.

3. That priests who wish to leave the active ministry be permitted to do so with dignity and honor.

4. That these proposals be presented by the representatives of the National Conference of Catholic Bishops of the United States to the Holy Father, Pope Paul VI, and the Synod of Bishops, convening in Rome on September 29, 1967.

5. That the implementation of these proposals be accomplished through the various national conferences of bishops.